Joseph Imagines God

A Philosophical Novel

By Roger Neumaier

This Book is dedicated to Bardwell Smith,
a wise man, a wonderful teacher.

Preface

The author is Jewish, the son of a Holocaust survivor who was an atheist. The author was raised in 1950's God-fearing America. He always wondered if there was a God and if so, what kind of God that might be. The following make-believe story is an extension of that curiosity.

1: Contact

My name is Joseph. The events in this story took place in 2009. I was married, a sixty-year-old county government chief financial officer. My wife and I lived in a charming, middle-class home. We had a lovely garden and three children who had grown up and left the nest. I was a typical guy. I watched baseball and football on TV, appreciated fine art and was pretty good at fixing things around the house.

*****

One spring day, I was at the office, working on an electronic spreadsheet, when the phone rang. I answered, "Hi, this is Joe. Can I help you?"

"Hi there. My name's Jeff Anderson. We haven't met. I reside here in the county. I'd like to set up a short meeting with you to talk about your priorities."

It wasn't unusual for me to receive a request to discuss the County's budget priorities. I maintained an open-door policy and a lot of county residents had strong opinions about how their taxes were spent. I had learned it's much better to have a dialogue with a citizen than to allow their concerns about county government to fester.

We agreed to meet the following morning.

*****

The next day Anderson arrived at my office promptly at ten. He was an older guy, dressed casually in a light blue button-down shirt and blue jeans. I invited him to sit at the small conference table in my office. For a few minutes, we made small talk about the economy and the challenges facing the local, state and national economies. During that conversation, I brought up the county's revenue streams telling him I was planning on reducing my projection for current year sales tax receipts. I explained this decision was based upon new collection trends that had been reported to me by the State.

After about five minutes of polite conversation, I told Anderson, "I have another meeting in a few minutes. Let me know your issue so that we are sure to address it before I get called into that next meeting."

Anderson responded, "I am asking something of you that will only require a limited amount of your time. It will turn out to be the most interesting offer you've ever received and will not put you or the County at risk"

I wasn't surprised by Anderson's statement. From time-to-time, a citizen or a vendor would come into my office offering to share their great idea for a sure-fire county investment or brilliant policy change. Once, a man suggested that our County construct a children's theme park—sort of like Disneyland. Another time, a visitor recommended I change the nation's currency back to the gold standard. Almost always, the ideas were half-baked, poorly conceived and not worth further consideration. But the goodwill that came out of paying attention to them was worth the time it took to listen.

"Mr. Anderson," I said, "I look forward to hearing your idea. But my time is limited. Let's go for it. What is your suggestion?"

Anderson handed me a sealed envelope and said, "Thank you for meeting with me, Joe. My proposal is explained in the letter in this envelope. Read it after I leave. It'll cover my proposal. I won't take any more of your time today."

That worked out well and we stood up and shook hands. As Anderson left my office, he turned toward me and said, "I'll give you a call at nine tomorrow to hear your response."

I returned to my desk, quietly laughing and shaking my head at what had just occurred. When I opened the envelope, there was a two-page letter inside of it. The letter began:

Joseph,

Thank you for taking the time to meet with me. I enjoyed hearing your thoughts about the economy. Your decision to reduce projected sales tax receipts based upon the report from the State Office of Financial Management is most prudent.

My attention was piqued. During our meeting, I told Anderson about having received information from the State about the local economy slowing down. But I hadn't mentioned that the Office of Financial Management had sent me that report. Even if Anderson had known about the letter before meeting with me, there was no way he could have been aware that I had decided to reduce revenue projections.

Anderson had been the first person to whom I'd mentioned that decision.

I shrugged my mental shoulders and continued reading the letter.

Please set aside your natural cynicism while you read this letter. You have just had a discussion that was different from any meeting you have ever had. You just met with God.

I laughed out loud. My assessment of Anderson was confirmed. He was a nut. I continued to read his letter.

I have always tried to help humans understand and cope with their life experience. From time to time, I have interceded—provided guidance to and for your species. Sometimes my objective was simply to share insights. At other times it was to deliver warnings. Those with whom I met were people of their time—full of the strengths and weaknesses of their historical period. But they were always able representatives of their respective civilizations who could effectively communicate with others within their tribes.

You are an honest and thoughtful person who has the capacity to understand the ideas I wish to transmit. You write simply and clearly—skills that will enable you to document my message so others will understand it.

I know you aren't particularly religious—I think you describe yourself as an agnostic. That is part of why I chose you for this conversation. I can't afford to waste my time with someone who is certain of their beliefs.

If you agree to meet with me, I require that you not discuss our communications with anyone until our meetings have been concluded and you have completed documenting our conversations. On that one rule, you must not break trust. I would be aware of such an action.

I propose a series of one-hour meetings in a public place. We would meet weekly beginning later this month. You would select a topic and questions for each meeting. I would speak to your topic and respond to your questions. After completing each session, you would summarize our conversations in writing. Later, you would refine that documentation and publish it.

Tomorrow morning, I will call you. At that time, I will respond to any questions you have about my proposal. Once I have responded to your questions, you can inform me whether you wish to move forward with my proposed arrangement. If so, we can set up our first meeting. If you are not interested in proceeding, you will not hear from me again.

No doubt, you have a lot of skepticism regarding whether my visit today was a hoax. This letter demonstrates the unique nature of my invitation. After you have completed reading the letter, read it again, fold the letter and place it back in the envelope. Then, take the letter out and reread it.

You will recognize the unusual nature of my proposal.

Yours truly,

God

*****

I sat at my desk, shaking my head and chuckling at the bizarre nature of Anderson's visit and letter. I had five minutes before my next meeting—time to reread the letter. I wouldn't have done that except for the letter's reference to the conversation about sales tax and the economy. That intrigued me. I was the one who had initiated the discussion of the economy because I believed Anderson was there to discuss our budget. I was curious how Anderson had anticipated that discussion in his letter. The envelope had to have been sealed before the meeting. If Anderson was a magician, he was a good one. If he was a hypnotist, he had done his work well.

I followed Anderson's instructions; folded the two-page letter; then placed it back into the envelope. A moment later, when I reopened the envelope and removed the letter, it had changed. Instead of a two-page letter, it had become a one-page, one-line note that simply said, *I will call you tomorrow.*

2: A Phone Call

After meeting with Anderson, I attended a budget presentation by the county sheriff, I wasn't able to focus as the sheriff struggled to explain, then justify his over-expenditures. I kept replaying the conversation with Anderson in my mind's eye. How had he pulled off changing his letter?

Back in my office, I pulled out the letter again. It was still only the one sentence. But the letter itself was confirmation that the meeting had occurred. I hadn't imagined it. I wondered, was it possible my work colleagues had set up the whole charade as a prank? Maybe my brother and sister had arranged it— with some magician—some guy who made his living pulling off this sort of gag?

The whole thing was surprisingly upsetting. I left the office early that afternoon—unable to take my mind off of Anderson and the letter. My wife was surprised to see me arrive home early. She asked me what was going on. I told her I had a troubling issue at work that I'd rather not get into. She let it go.

*****

I went out for a walk. It was a typical northwest spring day—cool, but pleasant. As I passed homes, I gazed at buds on ornamentals that were beginning to swell. But I wasn't thinking about those plants. I repeatedly asked myself the same questions: *Was I going to hear from this character again? Could this be anything other than a prank? Was I at risk?*

I replayed each of Anderson's statements in my mind. Were there any obvious hints of a prank in his two-page letter? I suddenly stopped walking. Maybe the envelope had a secret compartment. Maybe there were actually two letters in it in the first place?

I took the envelope out of my pocket and examined it. The envelope had no unusual compartments and the only thing in it was that one-page, single statement letter.

*****

I may have been full of doubt, but accountants get paid to be objective and attack tasks. That evening, those objective skills took over. I moved into a formal analytic mode. If Anderson actually did call me the next day, what questions should I ask?

I pondered that for a few minutes, then wrote down four questions.

Why should I believe what Anderson says?

How was I picked?

What was Anderson's objective in having these interviews?

Why shouldn't I believe this is a trick, a con or some sort of crime in the making?

*****

I didn't sleep well that night. I began to think about my religious beliefs and couldn't stop. What did I believe? How did I come to those beliefs?

Both my father and mother were Jewish. My dad escaped to the United States from the horror of Nazi Germany. His mother, my grandmother, along with many of my father's uncles, aunts, cousins and friends, perished in the Holocaust.

My mother's grandmother and two of my mother's uncles lived in a small Romanian shtetl. In the early 1940's, Nazis took the three of them from their shtetl into a nearby forest and murdered them.

My father had told me more than once that if there was a real God, he would not have allowed the atrocities the Nazis perpetrated.

That night, these and similar thoughts kept running through my mind as I tried to sleep.

*****

The following morning, I was in my office when the phone rang. I answered, "Hi, this is Joe. How can I help you?"

I recognized the voice. "Good morning, Joseph. This is Jeff Anderson. I'm following up on our talk."

While I was asking myself, *why am I even considering this,* the words out my mouth were, "I have a few questions for you about your proposal."

Anderson said, "That makes sense. Go ahead. Ask."

"OK," I started out, "Why should I believe you— even for a second?"

Anderson's response was given in a matter-of-fact manner. "Nothing I'm going to say today will make you believe that I am God. In fact, if you believed me without reservations after that brief visit, you would be proving that you are too naive to do what I ask."

"Let me give you a better question to ask," he said. "Why should you waste your time on something that logic tells you is either based on a lie or is a sign you are losing your mind? If you want me to respond to that question, I will."

I responded sarcastically, "Go ahead, Jeff. Make my day."

"You will meet with me, Joseph, because you are curious. You've never been offered anything so intriguing. What I've offered has captivated your imagination. Perhaps I am a fraud? But if you don't meet with me, you'll never know. You'll always wonder—maybe there was something to learn—something special—an opportunity missed. And my letter—the things about it that you cannot logically explain—it intrigues you so much that you'll never forgive yourself if you pass on my offer."

Anderson let his words sink in, then added, "Let me go ahead and respond to your other questions."

I had not shared my other questions with him. This, I thought to myself, will be interesting.

"I chose you for several reasons. First of all, I've read your financial and operational analyses. I'm impressed by your ability to be both comprehensive and objective. And you write succinctly. You allow readers to move past rhetoric into the ideas you wish to convey."

Anderson kept going. "Joseph, you're an honest person. A dishonest person would manipulate this opportunity for personal gain. Her or his product would not be believable. And if you had a big ego, you'd embellish my comments, treating your role as license to speak on my behalf. That is the last thing I want. Your humility makes me confident you would focus on what I wish to communicate."

He paused and the tenor of his voice changed from trying to convince me of something to explaining it. "Throughout history, I've offered perspectives and guidance to the human race. My communications were intended to help human beings understand the nature of their challenge. People, not those to whom I spoke, but their contemporaries and generations that followed, distorted my ideas, treating my message as an opportunity to create power structures for themselves. They ended up seriously distorting my message."

My secretary poked her head in the door, "Your meeting will start in a few minutes."

I put my hand over the phone speaker and said, "I'll be ready in five. Tell them to wait."

Anderson wasn't done. "Being a second-generation Holocaust survivor gives you a valuable perspective on the challenges human beings face. The fact that your family had to accept humanity's inhumanity will cause you to pay close attention to what I say, to ask questions others might not ask. I want that sort of attention paid to my words. That you are a Jew means nothing in and of itself. Jews are no more the chosen people than are atheists, aboriginals, Christians, Muslims, Buddhists, Hindi, or any other group of believers or non-believers. The fact that you are an accountant is a potential distraction. It is not my intent to give financial or economic insights. However, as an accountant, you have also developed a discipline for objective communication of information. That is a prerequisite."

As he finished his statement, I looked over my list of questions. He had not convinced me this wasn't a scam. He hadn't even tried. But his next statement did take that issue straight on.

"I understand you are concerned that this is a trick—that I am a fraud. Your cautious distrust is prudent. The only way to find out whether I am a con-artist is to participate in these meetings. You will decide whether that is the case based upon what you hear."

His responses had been reasonable, succinct and complete—but hardly overwhelming. The reason I was taken aback was not because he had given extraordinary responses. I had difficulty dealing with the fact that he had somehow responded to each of my planned questions—without my asking them. How had he anticipated them?

My secretary came to the door. "You gotta go now, Joe. They're waiting for you."

I told her I'd be out in a second. Anderson was silent, waiting on the phone while I considered my options. Of course, Anderson wasn't God. While I had no idea what trickery he had used to read my mind, I had no doubt that it was some sort of deception. Still, he was right. My curiosity had been fully engaged. I needed to figure out how he had done it. I was hooked. Asking additional questions would be an absurd exercise. I needed to give an answer.

"OK. You've responded to my questions. I don't believe you are God, but I will meet with you. However, I need to protect myself. I want these meetings to occur in a highly public setting—where I am not at risk. When and where will we meet?"

Anderson didn't hesitate. "Our meetings will be seven one-hour interviews on consecutive Sundays. The first one will take place at the city's public library. Be in the library's lobby a week from Sunday at eleven. Subsequent interviews will also be on Sundays at eleven. Write up your questions in advance of the interviews. And oh—you will not be able to record my voice, even if you try. So, bring a good pen and plenty of paper."

My secretary was standing in my office doorway looking anxious.

I started to say goodbye to Anderson, when he spoke again. "One other thing, the person you saw yesterday, the physical presence you perceived—it was an illusion. The person you see when we meet—the body, face and voice—they'll be different for each meeting."

I asked the obvious question: "Then how will I know it's you?"

I heard Anderson chuckle. "I'll let you know."

After that, Anderson said *so long*. As I rushed to my meeting, I felt foolish. Every instinct told me I had just committed to a course of action that was stupid and would later be regretted.

Yet Anderson had been right about one thing. I was awfully curious. And we all know—curiosity killed the cat.

3: Reflection and Preparation

As I drove home that evening, I reflected on a conversation I had had with my father a year after I graduated from college.

I was living and working at an upstate New York resort. It was about twenty miles from my father's home. I had visited my dad that Sunday afternoon and he was giving me a ride back to the resort via a picturesque route. As the road curved through the Shawangunk Mountains, my dad was speaking about his beliefs. He told me the reason he was an atheist was because, if there had been a real God, the Holocaust would not have occurred; so many innocent people would not have been murdered; and his mother might still be alive. After he said that, the road curved to the west taking us over a mountain ridge. A valley stretched out before us. Lights from homes at the far edge of the valley twinkled in the dusk. Against the sky, the pink and orange colors of the setting sun created a silhouette out of the mountains.

My dad looked at that stunning sunset, stopped speaking for a moment, then added, "But you know; I still can't get over how incredible the whole thing is."

I remember that conversation vividly. My father had always been so adamant that he did not believe in God. His comment—*how incredible the whole thing is*—speaks to what I believe is a primary reason people believe in God; an innate response to the extraordinary universe around us.

*****

15

Even though I doubted the meetings with Anderson would be fruitful, if I was going to take any task, I would do it well. I needed to pay attention to the structure of the interviews in the off-chance that the meetings might produce anything of value. I had ten days to put together a series of questions for Anderson. By the time I got home, I had figured out the approach I would take in identifying my questions.

During my career, whenever I had to analyze a complex issue, I would begin by putting together one list of the things I knew and a second list of the things I didn't know. Those two lists formed the context for my analysis. This was the approach I had decided to utilize in preparing for Anderson.

For the next three days, I spent a couple of hours each evening developing the two lists. The whole affair may have been a fantasy—but it was an intriguing fantasy and the exercise of developing its conceptual framework was stimulating.

I narrowed down the list of things I knew to the following:

Anderson claimed to be God.

He referred to persons for whom he was God as *humanity*—not focusing on any specific religious or national group. From that, I concluded he claimed to be one God for all peoples.

He said he would have a different presence for each interview implying he was not tied to a single physical identity.

He stated he wanted to provide guidance to humanity.

My list of things I didn't know could have been endless. But I screened out many items. Below is my final list of things about Anderson that I did not know:

What special powers he might claim to have.

The type of deity he would claim to be. Would he be an angry God, a loving God or possibly the devil?

If he would implicitly or explicitly favor one group of people, one race, one religion or one nationality above others.

If he would claim that there were other Gods.

If he would claim to be a God only for humans or whether he was the all-powerful for every living being.

If he would claim a connection with historical religious stories like those about Jesus, the Hindu Brahma or Moses.

What sort of guidance he proposed sharing with humanity? (If he wanted me to do something like build a boat and put two of every animal on it, it would be a giveaway that he was a real nut).

What he would say was the reason for his existence, why there was a universe, or what reason he might give for the creation of human beings.

Whether a single thing he had said to me about himself had been the truth.

*****

Over the years, I had learned how to create a well-defined structure for diverse assignments.

Creating themes and questions for these interviews, however, promised to be an especially interesting and unusual task. How often does one consider the essential themes for questions one would ask about the source of one's own being?

There would be seven question areas—one for each week's interviews. I wrote, revised, reordered and reworded my list until I had settled on seven major areas of questions.

My final list was:

What is God? What existed before God?

How was the universe formed and what was its purpose?

What is life? Is there a soul or an afterlife?

What is the value of religion?

How, when, and why had God communicated with mankind in the past?

What is the purpose of art?

What is humanity's future?

I identified follow-up questions for each week's theme. Their use would be driven by the approach Anderson took in responding to that week's primary question.

An almost competitive attitude emerged during my preparation. I had the skills to challenge superficial responses to my questions and was fully prepared to utilize those skills. I was going to push this con-artist.

*****

On the Saturday evening before our first meeting, I sat in my study reviewing the questions one last time. I chuckled to myself. "If Anderson believes he is going to receive simplistic questions and then get a free pass after giving me shallow responses, he has seriously under-estimated me."

4: What is God—What existed before God?

I entered the library Sunday morning and sat down on a bench in the lobby. It was eleven and I was alone in the lobby. Several minutes later, I was approached by a librarian with silver-grey hair pulled back into a bun. I wondered if she was going to give me a message from Anderson. Maybe he would be a no-show.

The librarian, who had was dressed in dark slacks and a white blouse, said in a grandmotherly tone, "Hi, Joseph. Today, you can call me Elenore. Are we ready to begin?"

My expectations were tossed asunder. I had expected Anderson to appear in some sort of disguise—maybe a fake beard or moustache. This was definitely not Anderson.

I hid my surprise and said, "Hi Elenore. Let's go for it."

With the confident steps of someone who had worked in that library for years, Elenore led me across the library's great room. We passed a student bent over homework and three older men leaning back in cushioned chairs while reading newspapers. Past the tall rows of shelves packed with books on the far side of the library's great room, was a door that led to a small conference room.

She opened the door and we entered the room. It was furnished with a solid oak table and six matching chairs. Across from the door, was a large window that looked out onto a city street. At one end of the room was a whiteboard. At the other end, was an oil painting of a small sailboat battling stormy seas.

That painting captured how I felt.

*****

Elenore closed the door, walked around the table and sat with her back to the window. After gesturing for me to take the seat across from her, she said, "I've looked forward to this conversation. I knew you would be structured in approaching these meetings and I am not disappointed."

Since I hadn't shared anything about my approach or themes with her—or anyone else for that matter—I figured she was either trying to intimidate me with her all-knowing power or just blowing smoke to flatter me.

Elenore wasted no time. "The areas you want me to address over the next few weeks are, of course, linked. I will respond to each of them. But first, I need to give you a word of warning. What I share will be challenging. You won't like what I say about the limitations of your capabilities or about your simplistic understanding of reality. Getting you to accept these shortcomings will be my greatest challenge. However, once you accept them, you will gain fresh insight into the world that is around you."

She paused. I was thinking, *OK, she's working to lower my expectations. Lady—relax. They are already low!*

Elenore gave me a patronizing smile. "As you know from your work, how you approach a question determines the answer you will reach. Humans have always had a jaded approach to answering the questions you've asked today. The Greek philosopher Protagoras stated, *Man is the measure of all things.* His pretentious (and sexist) remark is typical of western philosophy."

"Hmmm," I thought to myself, "Big words. Little meaning."

Elenore chuckled, then said, "Protagoras did not create that simplistic idea—he just repeated it. Human philosophies have almost always assumed that human beings can accurately perceive the universe. Few philosophers or scientists have bothered to explore the important distinction between what they perceive and what exists."

She looked at me, giving me moment to respond if I wanted. I said nothing and she continued. "I started out with Protagoras' statement because in order to accurately respond to your question, I must point out the serious problem with the perspective of his statement. An accurate restatement of Protagoras' words would be *Man believes he is the measure of all things.*"

I maintained a poker face, but I was thinking, *even though this sounds profound, it isn't responsive to my question at all. Elenore is putting on a show that has no relevance to what I asked. She doesn't have a clue what my question is. She is a fraud—an accomplice of Anderson who at best, is a mediocre con-artist.*

Elenore gave me a perplexed look, but kept speaking. "In the first book of the bible, a statement is made that is even more high-handed than the one by Protagoras. You've heard it many times: *God created man in God's own image.*"

At this point, Elenore's speech slowed down. "Before responding to your inquiry—*What is God*, it is necessary to explain the contextual fallacies humans generally make in trying to address your question. These fallacies are superbly on display in both the statement by Protagoras and the quote from Genesis. Implicit in both is that human beings have a primary role in the universe."

She took a deep breath and sighed. "In order for you to know God, you must abandon that egotistic and simplistic view of the world. Man was not created in God's image. The exact opposite is true. Humans created the God they worship in their own image. The God they created, Joseph, is a complete fantasy."

Even though she was speaking slowly, it was difficult to follow her ideas at the same time as I took notes. But I paid attention because I didn't want to miss any logical games she employed in moving toward what I was sure would be a superficial conclusion.

Fortunately, Elenore stopped speaking for a moment, giving me time to catch up.

Once I caught up, I looked at her and she continued. "A more useful question for you to have asked would have been, what do you, Joseph, have to do to eliminate your fantasy of human importance in order to gain insight into what God is? The answer to that question begins with letting go of the naive belief that you and other humans can accurately perceive the world around you. The truth is that human perceptive skills are extremely basic. As a result, their understanding of what is around them is simplistic. In order to understand God, you must accept—humans will have to accept—that the universe is much grander and more complex than they have the capacity to perceive."

Elenore stood up and walked to the end of the table. She began to pace back and forth as the meter of her lecture increased. I had a professor in college who used to do that. His students had to scramble to keep up. I always thought that professor spoke quickly so we couldn't daydream. I assure you, as I listened to Elenore, I wasn't daydreaming. She may have looked gentle; her voice might have been soft; but this little old lady was moving through ideas quickly. I had to scramble to keep up.

"In his allegory of the cave," Elenore continued, "Plato addressed the limitations in a human's ability to perceive. The basic theme of that allegory was that humankind has as little understanding of the world as a person who was placed at birth in a cave. That cave dweller had to learn about the nature of the world by watching shadows of reality—produced by a fire—on the irregular walls of the cave. I gave Plato the inspiration for that allegory. Unfortunately, Plato was also an egotist. He chose to expand the simple story, going on to describe the world as he imagined it, rather than taking to heart the humility called for by the metaphor. In so doing, Plato's arrogance caused him to display the weaknesses that the allegory was designed to highlight."

I stopped writing notes and looked up. It hit me that Elenore was totally focused upon challenging human perception capabilities rather than on responding to my questions. I wasn't going to let her get away with that sort of evasion.

I asked sarcastically, "Tell me Elenore, with all your understanding of everything, why can't mankind perceive the universe better?"

Instead of seeming to be offended by my tone, Elenore smiled—surprisingly warmly. "Fair question," she said. "I'll put it to you in simple terms. You and your species are limited by your basic tools of perception. Your capabilities to see, hear, smell, taste and touch do not allow you to perceive much that is going on in the complex universe that surrounds you. This situation is exacerbated by human arrogance. Humans find it difficult to accept limitations."

I interrupted again. "I get that you believe that. But you are offering a circular argument. You say I cannot perceive anything because I cannot perceive anything. If your goal is to help me understand the world, you need to offer more than a tautology and criticism of my ability to perceive the universe."

Elenore stopped pacing, turned to me, and said, "I will offer much more than that. But it won't be done today. Accepting the limitation of your capabilities, and by inference, all human beings' weaknesses in perceiving the universe—that is the greatest barrier you will face during our meetings. It is not easy for anyone to accept as a truth anything that is beyond their experience. And Joseph, there is so much beyond your experience—so many things you do not perceive. But before we complete our meetings, I believe you will accept this limitation and begin to have insight into how you can discover truth despite that constraint."

I had to give Elenore credit. She was patient, persistent and not easily offended. Still, my doubts about her and Anderson had not diminished. I felt that if what I had heard so far was indicative of what I could expect in the rest of our meetings; if she continued to make grand statements, but avoid backing them up; these meeting with Elenore, Anderson, or whomever else showed up would end up being a waste of my time.

Elenore continued her diatribe against human capabilities. "I could simply point out the weakness in your perceptive skills by asking if you know what the three men who were reading newspapers in the library's grand room had had for breakfast. My guess is you wouldn't have a clue. But, if a dog had walked through that main reading room this morning, the dog would know what each old man had eaten for breakfast. That is one small example of how your perceptive skills are worse than a dog's. Such an example doesn't touch upon the fact that that you are able only to hear, smell, taste, touch, and see—just five

of the multitude of senses required for complete
perception in the universe. But if I simply relied on
that comparison to a dog, you would be offended and
would gain no insight into what I am trying to tell you.
No, my most effective tools for bridging your
perception and comprehension limitations will not be
sarcasm. It will be the use of parables and metaphors,
simple stories that illustrate truth. Next week, I will
give you a parable that addresses the limitations of
human perception."

*****

Our meeting seemed like a television serial for
which viewers expect an issue to be resolved at the end
of an episode, but learn toward the end of that week's
show that the issue won't be resolved until the
following week's episode.

Elenore took another deep breath and exhaled.
"Before I start using metaphors and parables, I need to
point out that humans often have treated these
illustrative stories as literal accounts of actual events.
While those with whom I speak do understand that
these are illustrative tales intended to communicate a
truth, broader audiences often miss the symbolism.
They come to believe the stories are records of
historical events."

I shook my head, unsure of sure where she was
going with this.

Elenore appeared to understand that reaction.
"Let me give you an example. Several millennia ago, I
shared a metaphor with an Egyptian priest that

compared dying to crossing a river into a different world. The story was intended to illustrate that when a person dies, something totally different begins. That priest understood the metaphor. But the others he explained it to didn't. Egyptians began to bury their dead with food for sustenance and a boat to transport the deceased to the Field of Reeds, the Egyptians' mythological afterlife. The convoluted metaphor was easy for the Egyptian people to understand. It just had no value. It helped no one comprehend what the universe is—or what God is. Religious leaders have missed the boat by peddling primitive stories like this to their congregations throughout history. Some of those stories were based on twisted versions of things I had once shared. Others were just original fantasies. But both added to humankind's confusion about God— and the universe."

*****

If Elenore spent the entire hour lecturing about human beings' inability to perceive and misunderstood metaphors from the ancient past, she would be able to avoid having to respond to my question. So, I decided to call her on the game she was playing.

"I am sorry," I said, "but I'm getting frustrated. You say I can't perceive the universe. I wanted to know why you said that. You told me you'll explain that next week—with a metaphor. I'm fine with a metaphor, Elenore. But wait—now you are saying that parables and metaphors are poor tools for explaining anything— even though that was how you were going to show me I can't perceive anything. This seems like a conceptual shell game."

Frustration had taken over for me. I was considering leaving the conference room. But I decided instead to try to get her to share something more relevant to my life than criticisms of ancient Egyptians.

I told her, "Your example, Elenore, of how metaphors are poor tools was an example from Egypt. I don't know or care that much about Egypt. If you have to give me a situation where people bastardized the meaning of parables or metaphors, why don't you try something a little closer to home—something which relates to my time—my world?"

Elenore pensively returned to her chair and sat down. She bent her head, elbows on the table, forehead rested on her open hands. A moment later, she looked up, smiled and said, "That's fair enough. How about this? Let's talk about the birth of Jesus. I know you're Jewish. But that's a story you are familiar with. Right?"

I nodded.

"OK," she said. "This simple story about a baby in a manger teaches humility, love of others and the importance of not judging a person's value by their power or wealth. Do you agree that these are worthwhile values to teach?"

I said, "Yes."

"Good," she said. "But over the centuries, this metaphor has been expanded while the lessons inherent in it have diminished. In your time and civilization, what small children are taught about Jesus often has no more value than an account of an actual boat taking dead Egyptians to the land of the dead. Over the centuries, the simple metaphor of a poor child, born to a homeless mother, being the son of God has been used to justify building some of the most expensive edifices in human history. Those monumental churches were funded by common folk who were struggling to feed themselves. And at the same time, a landed aristocracy—the priests—emerged. The wealth of the church and its hierarchy is the antithesis of the humility that the story of Jesus was originally intended to teach."

"OK," I said. "I get your point about the story of Jesus and the manger. But Elenore, your only focus seems to be on the limitations of human perception and humanity's inability to appropriately utilize your prior metaphors. You've postponed until next week any explanation of your insinuation that mankind's perceptive skills are weak; and you haven't even begun to respond to my question: *What is God?* All you have done is complain about human incompetency."

Elenore didn't look at all pleased with my statement. After taking a deep breath, she replied, "As you stated, I committed to illustrate the limitations of human perceptive capabilities next week. At that time, I will explain why those shortcomings are such a basic part of human confusion about God. And yes, I have criticized humans' understanding of their place in the universe. But Joseph, I am giving you fair warning that I will not be describing a God that was created in the image of humans. You must understand that the image of a man with a long white beard—or anything similar to it—must be set aside before you will be able understand anything about the universe or about God."

She looked intensely at me as she continued, "I described how my past communications have been manipulated so that you will better understand the challenge you face. Even if you come to understand and accept what I will share with you over these next few Sundays, you will have difficulty documenting it in such a way that others do not manipulate your words into just another set of meaningless myths. You face a challenge in producing a document that does not become just another base for fantasy while giving some people false comfort and others power."

*****

Elenore paused and looked at me. The intensity of her gaze threw me off. "I know you are frustrated," she said. "You want a simple answer to your question."

She was right but I was taken aback by the directness of her response. I began to feel embarrassed by the disrespect I had exhibited. My face flushed. I had been wrong about one thing. Elenore was good— really good. For a moment, I thought that maybe there was something more to this than a con-job. But I quickly pushed that thought out of my mind and returned to taking notes. I also determined that I needed to avoid letting my facial expressions telegraph thoughts that would end up embarrassing me.

"Let's dive into your question," she said. "*What is God?* I will give you a concrete description and a metaphor. At this point, the description will not help you understand too much. But if you write it down and study it, it might make some sense later on. Does that work for you?"

I gave a half-hearted *yes*.

Elenore nodded. "OK. The concrete description first: God is the conscious tension within unlimited space that gives cohesion to the universe. God is the design, the structure, the intent, and the energy that ties all physical and psychic phenomena into a meaningful and evolving order. God is both the order and the reason there is order in the universe."

I wrote this down verbatim and looked up. I must have looked confused because Elenore changed her approach.

"Maybe it would be more useful for me to tell you what God is not. God is not a he—not a she. God is not a moral judge nor does God watch over flocks of people. God doesn't make judgments or decisions in order to micromanage the universe. God, the judge, is a fictitious extension of humanity's systems of controlling one another. It is not an accurate description of God."

She paused, then slowly said, "God is not one being—nor is God several. God is a continuum."

I wasn't sure what Elenore meant by describing God as a *continuum*.

Though I had said nothing, Elenore responded as if I had asked her to clarify her statement. "OK, Joseph. When describing the lakes, rivers, and oceans of the world—would you say there is *one body of water* or *many individual and unique waters?*"

I waited, figuring that this might be a rhetorical question.

As it turned out, that was the right call because Elenore answered her own question. "The answer is both. Water is a continuum. It is one and it is many. God has more in common with water than with humanity."

I thought about what she had said for a moment, then responded, "I got it."

She nodded and continued. "Good. In order to understand God, you will have to change another major paradigm. God is not the creator of the universe. God did not, at some point, create the universe out of a black hole. God did not magically produce men and women. The fantasy of human creation is driven by humanity's need to declare their own importance."

Elenore was silent for a couple of minutes before stating, "Joseph, the God defined by humans does not exist. God is not the designer of the universe— nor its builder. But God does exist. God is the order and the underlying focus that makes the universe a whole rather than many disparate pieces. No, God is not the designer. God is the design."

As I wrote down those words, I realized it would take some time after our meeting to determine whether they were just rhetoric, or really made any sense.

Elenore waited until I caught up in my notes before she spoke again. "Here is the metaphor I promised. It's the same metaphor I shared with Lao Tzu. I referenced it a moment ago. God is like water. Water has many powers. It is necessary for plants to grow and it can quench human thirst. It can transport people. Even though water can be soft to the touch, it becomes rigid in cold temperatures and seem to disappear into a vapor when heated. Water can cut through rock formations. It causes natural disasters or stop wildfires. Water can be so many different things in so many different circumstances that defining it is an elusive task. But while water can demonstrate so many different powers, it is absolutely consistent and predictable."

She paused, watching me write. After I looked up, she said quite emphatically, "One thing water does not do is make conscious decisions. While it can be punishing, water does not consciously punish—anything or anyone. But water demands respect from human beings. Those who mistreat water suffer severe consequences. If you perceive conservation of water—the preservation of nature—as a natural moral law with consequences, you have a better idea of God than if you regularly visit a house of worship and prostrate yourself to ask for forgiveness from the Lord."

*****

Then Elenore began to speak slowly again. "As you learned in Sunday school, the ancient Hebrews did not have a word for God. Instead, they used words which expressed respect. By not assigning a name to God, the Hebrews avoided implying knowledge of God. That practice was established by Abraham's—driven by his humility—his recognition of his own—of humanity's—limitations. Abraham's humility was the cornerstone of his wisdom. In asking me to tell you what God is, you have requested what Abraham understood was unattainable. Does it reflect well upon your wisdom that a primitive man—thousands of years ago—grasped what you cannot get your arms around today?"

*****

Elenore stopped. When I caught up in my notes, she asked me, "Have I responded to your request?"

I paused, a little taken aback. I realized that if I didn't respond now, I couldn't complain later. "I have listened to what you've said, Elenore. But I'll have to spend some time in the coming week going over your concrete description. It may be correct, but it's a little like a mathematical formula—hard for me to visualize. And as far as the metaphor of water goes, I get it. Nice metaphor. But, to be honest with you, while you may think you have answered my questions, I don't think you have. You warned me that what you shared would not conform to my expectations. In that you were correct. But I could label both your metaphor and your concrete definition as skillful avoidances of a direct answer. If this is the best you can do, these meetings might turn out to be a waste of time."

"Thank you for your honesty," she said. "I wish I could make this simple for you. But understanding God will not be a small thing. Even though my definitions may not conform to your expectations, this is the way it is. God isn't, nor will God ever become, a wise old man sitting in the clouds. *What is God?* is arguably the most difficult question you will ask. All of the rest of your inquiries fall out of, and complement, that one question. And all of my answers will tie together in responding to it. Many of the things that will help you understand what God is are tied to questions we will discuss in the coming weeks. You will be in a better position to say *yes, you understand* or *no, it's not working* after our last meeting rather than now, in the midst of our first."

My confidence had not increased. But I had been honest about my reservations. I shrugged my shoulders and said, "OK. Go ahead."

*****

Elenore gave me a gentle, kindergarten teacher smile and said, "So in order to move forward, it sounds like you would like me to give you—for now—a simpler working definition of God. If we can do that, I have no doubt that later on you will be able to get your arms around the larger concept. Now, this definition will be simple, not simplistic. *Simple* can be augmented. I can add and expand upon *simple* in future meetings. *Simplistic* is a dead end. *Simplistic* is an old man with

36

a beard on a throne who manages humanity like a—well, like a kindergarten teacher."

I smiled and said, "Fine. Go for it. Give me simple."

"OK," she said as she returned me smile. "Let's start with this: God is multi-faceted order. God—not a he nor a she—is here for all living beings in the universe—not just for humans. Next, I'll add that God's intent is that each being seek harmony in their life. We'll speak a lot more about harmony later. But for now, I'll simply say that God wants all living things to pursue harmony. That's manageable, isn't it?"

I nodded affirmatively. But it seemed to me that Elenore's definition of God was sort of light-weight. Maybe it was intellectually defensible, but if she couldn't give me a more useful definition of God, well, it just didn't bode well for the rest of the interviews.

Elenore stopped speaking and gave me a look, shook her head and sighed. "That, Joseph, is a simple, workable definition of God. You asked for it. However, even if you did understand and accept the more complex concrete description which I offered earlier, you wouldn't know what God is. Please try to be patient. You will understand all of this better later on."

She turned away, and looked out the window. After catching up on my notes, I put down my pen and joined her in looking at the street. I was surprised how tired I felt.

Out on the pavement, a couple of young girls were riding bicycles. One of them lifted both hands off of her handle bars. A moment later, her bicycle wobbled and the girl began to lose her balance. She quickly grabbed her handlebar with one of her hands, stabilizing her bike. I remembered doing the exact same thing when I was a kid. It was a sweet memory.

*****

I looked back at Elenore and realized she had been studying me. She gave a warm smile and asked if I was ready to continue.

"Yes," I said. "I appreciated the break."

She smiled again before saying, "You are also asking me to tell you what existed before God."

"I am," I said.

"That question is grounded in two flawed concepts, Joseph. One of those flaws is your concept of time. The human concept of time is a sequential linear system, an extension of your serial perception of events. I won't attempt to explain the full nature of how events are linked to one another today. We'll get to that on another Sunday. But suffice it to say, events are linked to one another in a much more complex structure than your perception of time reflects."

She was silent for a moment before continuing. "Creation myths begin with a god creating the universe—one way or another. The example you are most familiar with begins, *On the first day, God created the heavens and the earth.* But what was there before creation? Has anyone thought about that? Did anything exist or happen before that creation? Without getting into the nuances of *infinity*, I can tell you that time—the progress of existence; the measure of events—time before the *first day* had to have lasted forever. If the time before creation lasted forever, then how could creation have occurred? An identical illogical fallacy exists in your question: What existed before God? I don't want to spend more time analyzing the whimsical, but you must realize that no one else has figured this one out either—for very good reasons."

"However, that absurd discussion is unnecessary because I can assure you, there wasn't a first day. The universe—and God—have always been there—will always be."

Elenore waited for that to sink in before saying, "And the other flawed concept upon which the proposition of God creating the earth depends, is mankind's visualization of God as a separate and distinct element from the universe rather than a fundamental quality of the universe. We will be speaking about that a lot on future Sundays."

I couldn't help but chuckle. While Elenore kept dumping on human intellect and capabilities, I liked her. She would have been a wonderful grade school teacher.

*****

Elenore stood up and walked to the far end of the room. She again began to pace again as she spoke. "We need to move beyond your question about the creation of God to a much more relevant question: Why do humans define God as an all-powerful being—

much like a human king endowed with magical powers?"

She looked at me and waited for a response. I said nothing.

Again, Elenore answered her own question. "We both know that humans often find life to be terrifying. Those who have the least amount of power frequently are the most threatened. They feel life is violent, arbitrary and unfair. They desire a benevolent protector; someone who can guard them from horrors that might be around the corner; someone they can easily visualize—a king of kings."

Her reference to a *king of kings* didn't appear to have been made with any sarcasm. She seemed to be speaking from the heart. Her face expressed compassion as she said, "Imagining a God who gives humans the ability to move forward in the face of fear and pain is understandable—perhaps even laudable. But the belief in a magical king is a fantasy designed for comfort rather than a true understanding of the universe."

She stopped speaking, pivoted away from me, and glanced out the window. After taking a huge breath, then letting it out slowly, she turned back to me and said, "I need to close out today's discussion of what God is by reiterating my most important point: There is a God—but that God is not the one imagined by humans. We will return to the question *What is God?* again and again during our meetings. In fact, every inquiry you make will require a response in the context of that question."

*****

Elenore was silent. I looked at my watch. It was noon. I wondered how I was going to feel about the meeting after reviewing my notes. Maybe some of it would end up making sense? Or maybe it was nonsense and I had just been worn down by her non-stop talking? I certainly hadn't answered my personal question of whether this was a prank or not. The only thing I was certain of was that I was tired—and hopeful that we were about to wrap up for the day.

"Before we conclude," she said, "I need to clarify one more issue that looms in front of you. It is deeply relevant to today's topic. Since our meeting in your office, in addition to wondering if I am a con-artist or whether you are losing your mind, you've occasionally wondered, *Might I really be meeting with God?* I know when I met you in your office, my letter said that you had just met with God. There was some truth in that. I am a face of God for you for a moment—a voice of God for you today and in our other interchanges. But I only serve as a window offering you a glimpse into truth. You must understand that having a glimpse of something or seeing an image that offers a taste of a thing—and knowing the nature of that thing itself—they are not at all the same."

*****

41

I attempting to digest that last statement as I wrote it down. The room had become silent—marred only by the noise of my pen on paper.

I looked up. Elenore was watching me. She smiled and said, "That was a good session. Come to the lobby, same time, next week. I will see you then."

I was taken aback and didn't respond. She smiled, walked around the table, opened the conference room door and left the room. I grabbed my pens and papers and followed her out of the room. Elenore was nowhere to be seen.

I walked out of the library and returned home.

5: How was the Universe Formed?

During the week that followed, I reviewed my notes from the meeting with Elenore. I wondered what her relationship to Anderson might be and analyzed countless oddities about the process that I had begun. A couple of times, I wondered if I was going a little crazy. Each time, I came back to the conclusion this was some sort of con-job. But what was their objective? Who was behind the whole scheme? I could write a chapter reviewing all of the possible explanations that ran through my mind. The only thing I was certain of was that I had not met with anyone supernatural because meeting with God is impossible.

Accountants are dependable. So, even though I had plenty of misgivings, I was diligent about transcribing the notes from the first interview and preparing for the second. I also put together a list of the things that Elenore had promised to clarify in upcoming meetings. I would hold her—them—accountable.

*****

As I entered the library on the following Sunday, I was focused on wiping raindrops off of my glasses. When I looked around, I saw I was alone. I sat down and waited, full of misgivings. Maybe participating in this process was a bad idea? Perhaps I should just leave—and go back home.

But I stayed there and waited, wondering if I had screwed up on the instructions for the day. Finally, I walked over to the conference room where I'd met

43

with Elenore the prior week. Maybe the would-be God would be there. The door was closed. I opened it a crack and peeked in. A middle-aged Asian man was sitting at the head of the conference room table. He gestured for me to enter the room.

In a Chinese accent, the man said, "Good morning, Joseph. I wanted to give you a few minutes in the lobby to consider what you are pursuing. Do you want to prove I am a fraud or are you interested in learning something? I am not sure you have resolved that conundrum, but I will proceed as if you decided you wanted to learn something. Please call me Mr. Lee."

What could I say? I shook Mr. Lee's hand, took a seat, and said, "Good morning, Mr. Lee. I'm all ears."

"Of course, you asked how the universe was formed," he began. "Every earth person I speak to is eager to learn the answer to that question. Modern people are as curious as those from ancient civilizations. Everyone wants to know, *How was the universe started*? After that, they ask, *What is the universe's purpose*? Their questions aren't driven by intellectual curiosity. Humans seem to need to hear that the universe's beginning and its purpose are focused upon humanity. Such a response validates their own importance. They like to hear something like *God created the earth in seven days and his crowning achievement was Adam and Eve*."

Lee chuckled. "All of the allegories about God creating the earth were invented by humans—every one of them—total fabrications," said Mr. Lee while looking down and shaking his head. "These myths were designed by humans to respond to their insecurity regarding their place in the universe. These myths that give comfort are based upon a multitude of human paradigms. One of those paradigms is that time is sequential and the universe was the start of that sequence. Of course, that is illogical. And, as I said last week, if that was the case, what existed before time—what existed before the universe?"

Mr. Lee allowed a moment of silence before continuing. "A second paradigm driving these creation stories is that God is focused on humanity—not just upon the species, but upon every individual human. That fantasy gives comfort to an individual—that he or she is never alone—and it seems to give meaning to a person's life (even if no one is certain what that meaning is). This paradigm also ignores all other life in the universe, a perspective that has no basis other than man's egotism. If you were to take the time to analyze any one of the allegories about creation, you would find it to be ludicrous. But because these fairy tales are about God, too few question them in the belief that questioning them would offend God."

When I caught up on my notes, I put my pen down for a moment and considered what Lee had just said. It was an interesting take—probably valid. But it occurred to me that once again, he was giving a critique of human beings rather than answers to my question. The week before, Elenore had promised that

45

this week, I would receive answers to some of my questions. I sat there waiting to see if that would occur—all but certain it wouldn't.

Lee sighed and said, "I want to put you in my shoes for just a moment, Joe. Can you appreciate the difficulty I have in describing something to you that is beyond what you are able to imagine?"

I pondered that question for a second. Then, partly just to hear what he had to say, I said, "OK. I'm not sure where you're going with this. But yes. For you to communicate to me the attributes of something I can't imagine would be a challenge."

Mr. Lee responded, "Thank you. What I am trying to tell you is that if you did comprehend the magnitude of the universe, you wouldn't ask me about its beginning."

Lee was telling me he couldn't answer my question about the universe's beginning because I didn't understand the universe. If he believed that to be the case, why not tell me something about the universe? I decided my best response would be to demonstrate that I did understand the universe.

"You're wrong, Mr. Lee. Maybe my understanding is limited, but I am not as ignorant as you are claiming. I know that the earth is large, a medium-sized planet in a larger solar system. I understand that that solar system is only a small part of a galaxy we call the Milky Way. The Milky Way is just a small part of a much grander universe. My understandings are based upon human perceptions, scientific observations and human logic. My comprehension may not be complete, but it represents some knowledge. You are wrong to state that I have no context for understanding the universe."

Lee rolled his eyes. "I know that you have absorbed the modern human understanding of the universe. Good for you. But if that understanding is seriously flawed, how would you know? What value would your understanding have? Last week, I promised to give you some insight into the weaknesses of your observation faculties. I referred to them as *humanities limited perception capabilities*. You were concerned that I would ignore doing this today. Well, your concerns were unfounded. I will proceed to share that insight."

My assumption had been wrong. But I had no confidence that any explanations he produced would have any value.

Lee stood up, placed his hands on the back of his chair, and leaned forward resting his weight on the chair. He looked directly at me as he said, "In order to help you understand these limitations, I must use a metaphor. This is a good time to repeat the warning I gave you last week. Even if a metaphor gives you insight into the ideas I am trying to explain, when you repeat that metaphor in your documentation of our meetings, others will try to take the metaphor out of context. They will use it for their own purposes. Of course, this is true of everything I share with you. I am

damned if I create a metaphor for you—and damned if
I don't."

Mr. Lee paused. A wry smile formed on his lips
as he added, "That's amusing—isn't it? I mean me,
using the phrase *I am damned,* in relation to myself.
It's actually funny."

From my perspective, Lee's joke fell into the
cute category rather than actually being funny and our
discussion was becoming more frustrating than the
prior week's with Elenore. If Lee was going to give me a
metaphor to make his point, he should do it.

*****

"I want you to imagine a scientist," Lee said,
"who is using a microscope. She is studying
microorganisms and enters data from her observations
into a computer database. The database program
which consolidates her inputs also organizes them into
groups of microorganisms. Sounds pretty typical,
doesn't it? But our scientist has a few problems. The
lens of her microscope is dirty and has a scratch. It
distorts what she sees and, as a result, she incorrectly
identifies some cells. And oh, our scientist occasionally
makes input errors as she types data into her
computer. To top it off, her database's analytics include
formulas with mathematical and logical flaws."

Lee paused, leaning forward and looking
directly at me. "My question for you, Joe, is how
credible will her conclusions be—given that they will be
based solely upon the database's reports?"

I waited a moment to make sure this was not a rhetorical question. Lee just looked at me and waited.

"I understand your metaphor." I responded. "Your point is that poor perception and faulty logic leads to useless conclusions. I don't need to be a rocket scientist to figure that one out. But I believe scientists' basic perceptions and analysis of the universe are not faulty. What would be useful would be a concrete example of human faulty perception or logic. Can you give me one specific example? How is human perception or logic so faulty that we cannot have insight into the world around us?"

Mr. Lee nodded. "Excellent request. I will be glad to do that. Your question for today has a simplistic and inaccurate foundation built on both how human beings perceive the universe and how they understand time."

"OK," I said. "That is what you said last week."

Lee smiled. "I can see you are an accountant. You believe in accountability and I will not disappoint you. I will give you a specific example of how your perception is much too simple for the complexity of the universe. Your question was: *When was the universe formed?* The question assumes a specific beginning of time. Humans alternatively call that *the creation* or *the formation of the universe*. Your understanding of time also assumes a single end point—today. Is this understanding correct?"

I paused, digested the question, then answered, "I guess so."

"For you, Joseph, time appears to be a simple straight-forward sequential phenomenon. Such a linear perception of time is fundamental to all human observations of experience. But the fact that all humans perceive their experience in a similar manner, does not make that manner accurate."

"That's true. But you still haven't told me how that manner is inaccurate."

"Time is not linear. It is not like a single piece of yarn stretched out across a room. Time is more like a ball of yarn—each point on that string of yarn touches, overlaps, and corresponds to other points on the string. Once this long piece of yarn has been wound into a ball, its beginning, is not at one end. The piece of yarn's beginning is found at the center of the ball. It winds out from that center point into to a large series of intermediate points. The center point is not such a great distance from any of the intermediate points. One could say that the beginning of the ball of yarn is at one of an infinite set of points inside the ball and its end is one of an infinite set of points on its exterior. My point is that time is not a straight line like a piece of yarn."

I wrote rapidly. Fortunately, Mr. Lee stopped speaking and let me catch up on my notetaking. When I looked up, he returned to his metaphor.

"Time is similar to a tightly wound ball of yarn," he said. "It is not a sequential collection of moments. Any one moment of time touches other moments of time. One time period crosses diverse other time periods. This collection of moments can be described as a *harmonic time construct*. It is beyond human capability to perceive time in this manner. Humans see time like a straight piece of string. They are not able to perceive or logically process all the ways in which moments of time intersect and correspond with one another."

Lee stopped speaking and was silent for a couple of minutes. During that silence, I considered the metaphor. I wondered if he was just blowing smoke in order to distract me from expecting a more serious response. I concluded I'd have to take a few hours considering the metaphor during the week that followed before deciding.

Lee continued. "Your paradigm about time precludes your accepting that there was no *creation of the universe* as you like to call it. Any attempt to describe the universe is inherently confused by that invalid perspective of sequential time. Any question you ask about the universe's beginning has as its foundation this invalid premise. It is impossible for me to give you an honest answer about the formation of the universe—that you will accept."

I was trying to get my arms around what Lee had just said. Then he zigged when I anticipated he would zag.

"There are many different ways to perceive time. Some are more simplistic than others. Viewing time as linear is not wrong. It is just so simplistic that it cannot be used as a foundation for a broad understanding of the nature of the universe. Thus, it isn't that humans are wrong when they speak about time in a linear fashion. It is just that their perspective is severely limited. It is inadequate for formulation of a more complete comprehension of the world around you. It is, to borrow from my previous metaphor, the proverbial dirty, scratched lens through which you attempt to see the universe."

Lee stopped speaking. He looked at me for a moment, then said, "This is where I need to warn you that leaning too heavily on the parable of the yarn as a means of understanding time (and the universe) would result in a whole new set of misconceptions. The yarn example is a metaphor. As such, it is not a complete or fully accurate description of time. Because of your limited ability to perceive, you—and the human race—cannot expect to comprehend everything. Once you accept how little you are capable of knowing, you will open the door to finding a path for greater insight into the world in which you live."

The grimace that must have appeared on my face was an expression of my frustration with what seemed to be useless answer.

Lee responded to the grimace. "I see your frustration. But you told me you are seeking the truth. Joseph, I don't think you do want to hear the truth. What you want is validation of your current beliefs. You want me to describe time in the manner you perceive it. But more importantly, you want to hear me speak about humanity with the reverence that you have ascribed to it. Unfortunately, I cannot do that."

He paused—probably to let that sink in. I took a deep breath and prepared for more criticisms and did not have to wait long to get them.

"You wonder why I criticize humanity—why I am so critical of you. Your problem is that you are not ready to change your assumptions about the universe. You are far too comfortable with your beliefs. In order to transmit to you an understanding of the way things are, I have to point out your faulty paradigms and be honest about human beings' inherent limitations. But Joseph, I have bad news. Those limitations are not limited to human perception and intellectual capabilities. Humans have much a larger problem. Most human beings don't have the humility required to compensate for their other inadequacies."

Talk about adding insult to injury! I was feeling defensive—and this on behalf of the human race! And Lee wasn't done dressing us down.

"In describing the inadequacy of the human understanding of time," he said. "I have merely scratched the surface of their inadequate perceptions, their lack of comprehension of the wider universe. There is so much beyond the concept of time for which human beings do not even have a glimmer of insight. Even if you, the recorder of my ideas, have the humility to accept these shortcomings, those who read your words will not only disagree, they will become angry with you. You will discover that the world is full of people who are unable to consider a fresh way of seeing because such a change would remove the feeling of security that is ensconced in their myths."

*****

Lee stopped speaking. You could have heard a pin drop in the conference room. I didn't know if the day's meeting was about to conclude. I looked out the window and considered what I had just heard. I tried to get my arms around its ramifications. It was clear that Lee was challenging the fundamental framework of how we humans see ourselves.

"As I said," he went on, "humans have constructed an understanding of the universe that is based upon an array of false paradigms. Time is only one of those problematic elements in their intellectual foundation. Another major misconception is that humans generally consider the physical world to be distinct from the psychic world. Physical and psychic phenomena are different aspects of the same moments—of the same points in space. If you had the capacity to perceive the full panorama of physical and psychic phenomena for only one moment, this would be laughably obvious."

Lee had lost me. "What do you mean?" I asked.

"Humans perceive sight, touch, sound, and smell and have a limited capability to occasionally glimpse what they refer to as psychic phenomena. They believe that they have seen all that can be perceived. Their conclusion is that there is little psychic activity in the universe. That, my dear friend, is a tautology. Because I do not perceive it, it cannot exist!"

This time, I was the one who chuckled. His point was good—and he was right—at least from a logical perspective.

Still, Lee wasn't done. "If you were sufficiently humble, if you accepted your shortcomings, you would accept that they there may be huge components of the universe—around you—that you cannot perceive. You would be ready to increase your understanding of the universe. But this is not the case with you—not the case with most humans. Your lack of humility, human beings' lack of humility, stands in the way of the ability to learn about—well, about life."

I interrupted Lee. "Let's say you're right for a moment. If I can't perceive anything more than what I see today, how can I learn? You rant about human beings' poor understanding of the universe. But you haven't told me anything about the way you say the universe really is. You certainly haven't made any effort to answer my question. Instead, you tell me that because my question is irrational, you don't need to give me any answer. It seems like you are telling me to forget everything I ever believed—that human beings should just accept they are ignorant beasts. Your single rationale, Mr. Lee, seems to be that we cannot know anything because we—the human race—are stupid, ignorant and blind."

I was surprised at my anger. It is not my style to lose my temper, but I had lost it. And I wasn't feeling one bit of regret for having lost it.

Lee asked, "Do you really believe that God created the universe as well as Adam and Eve in less than a week?"

I said nothing.

"Does it make sense to you that outer space ends? What is on the other side of that end to outer space? A McDonalds Restaurant? Do you really believe that the universe was created at a point in time? If so, what preceded that point in time?"

Lee waited for me to speak. I said nothing. I didn't have an answer. He had made his point.

In a softer tone, Mr. Lee said, "I know you are a smart man, Joseph. What I would like you to do is not view our conversations as a debate. Go ahead. Ask questions. I'll answer them. Call me out when you feel my logic is faulty. I'll respond. At the end of our seven weeks, you may decide that all of what I have said is garbage. In that case, just forget about documenting our conversations. But if that is the course you choose, what will you believe about the universe? Will your belief system rest on a magical creature up in the sky who created everything or will you believe that in some way, the universe has existed forever and there is no order other than existence? Aren't those really the alternatives? The big bang theory is a weak attempt to explain your world. If you believed it, I would ask you, *what existed before the big bang?*"

Lee paused, looked at me, then continued in the same gentle tone. "If you decide that things existed forever, Joseph, will you believe that there is any meaning in life—any rhyme or reason—at all? You tell me. You can end these discussions now if you wish. Just tell me. Take off. Walk out of the room. If you are satisfied that there is nothing to learn here—or better yet, if you feel that you are satisfied with your understanding of the world, then goodbye. Enjoy yourself."

I was calming down. Lee's approach was working. I was listening. Of course, he was right. In two months, if I wanted, I could just forget about these interviews. The only down-side would be a few lost Sunday mornings and a few dozen hours wasted in my study. I would be able to go ahead with my life and forget all that had been said to me by Anderson, Lee and Elenore.

"Go ahead," I said. "You're right. I don't need to make any decisions now. But I warn you, I might do exactly that—I might just forget about all of this and chalk our meetings up as a big waste of time."

*****

Lee gave me a friendly smile and returned to his lecture. "So where were we. Oh, yes, you were thinking, *He avoids giving me any real insight into the nature of the universe by just criticizing humans.* Well, I think I did give you an answer and it was quite simple. The universe was not created. It simply exists. It always has."

The expression in Lee's voice increased and he began to gesture with his hands as he spoke. "The universe is dynamic, Joe, constantly moving, always changing on multiple levels. It is continuous motion. It's always been that way, Joseph—always. It doesn't have a beginning—nor will it have an end. I know that response is not satisfying like the fantastic creation myths humans create. And it certainly offers no reassurance that humans are special—that they have a special guardian in the sky. But, Joe, it does offer one advantage. It is the truth."

He looked at me with an almost affectionate warmth as he said, "Stories like the one you told your daughter when she was small—when she woke up in the middle of the night, afraid of the sound of frogs—those stories give reassurance—even if they are fantasies that do not explain the universe."

I was startled by Lee's reference to my daughter and the story of the frogs. When she was small, my daughter would sometimes wake up crying in the middle of the night. I would go to her bedside and tell her stories until she fell asleep. One spring when she was four-years-old, she was awakened by frogs croaking in a pond on our rural property. Because she'd never heard the loud croaking sound, my daughter was afraid. I told her the sound came from the frogs in our pond. They had just woken up after a long winter's sleep. They were celebrating their awakening by telling one another, *We like mud. We like mud. We like mud.* That simple make-believe tale had calmed her. It explained something that had been frightening. After hearing the story, she smiled, rolled over and fell asleep.

I stopped taking notes for a moment while remembering that story created for my daughter so many years before. Lee waited. He was silent. I looked up and saw he was watching my reaction.

After a minute, he said, "Humans have always tried to understand the purpose of the universe with their intellect. But intellectually understanding the universe—or any part of it—is beyond human reach. In order for you to come closer to comprehending the universe, you must behave more like one of the frogs in your pond. You must sense that you are an organic element in the universe rather than a superior being trying to intellectually abstract its purpose. You should behave more like the frogs who embraced the universe as they croaked in the night."

Lee's pace slowed down. "I know you want me to give you an answer that is more definite than this. You want something similar to how you would describe the use of a tool you might purchase. You want a clear answer—something like *the purpose of a vacuum cleaner is to clean the floor. Likewise, the purpose of the universe is to....*"

Lee chuckled. "But I can't give that sort of answer. If I did, it wouldn't be the truth. Such an answer doesn't exist. Instead, I suggest you give more thought to the simple elegance of the frogs in the pond. Absorb some of their humility. Once you do that, you will understand more about the universe than you do now."

Mr. Lee allowed another moment of quiet. I was unsure of how to proceed. Again, I wondered if the day's interview was over.

But Lee had more for me. "So how does God fit into the universe? In order for you to understand who I am—what God is, I'll offer you an easy question: Do you believe in Santa Claus?"

I didn't think that question had any value. It felt like it had been offered in a patronizing tone and I looked up, sarcastically saying, "No. I don't."

Lee quickly retorted, "Why don't you believe in Santa Claus? You certainly have no proof he does not exist. You might say, *I can prove he doesn't exist. Parents purchase gifts for their kids.* That would only prove that the version of Santa Claus, that wase defined by you and by other humans, does not exist. True?"

I think I rolled my eyes before saying, "OK."

"I am not saying Santa Claus exists, Joseph. But you don't know that he doesn't. You just know that Santa Claus does not exist in the way parents have described him to their children. Because Santa Clause does not meet your definition, you believe he is a fantasy. God has been defined for humanity in a manner that is very much like Santa Claus—and I might add, by some of the same people who invented the story of Santa Claus."

Lee looked directly at me when he asked, "Why am I talking to you about Santa Claus? Because like stories about Santa Claus, most descriptions of God are fairy tales—as also happens to be the case with fables about formation of the universe. God, as typically described by humans is a fantasy. But Joe, God does exist. However, not as the puppeteer overseer of the universe. Instead, God is the way of harmony within the universe; the design that ties together animate and inanimate objects; a pervasive rhythm across the universe that is fundamental to all life."

This intensely condensed description of God appeared to be worth pondering. But I didn't have the time to absorb it because Lee kept speaking and I had to keep writing. I would have to spend time trying to better understand that description during the week that followed.

And Lee was on a roll. "Part of the reason most people have no understanding of God or the universe is because they have been preached at about God and the universe based upon the whimsical myths that we have already discussed."

"What will it take to open mankind's eyes?" he asked. "In order to learn about God and the universe, human beings will have to let go of their comfortable fantasies. Those fables insulate humans from curiosity. Removing their fantastic stories of a loving god won't be easy. It would mean humanity would also have to let go of the concept of their race as the pinnacle of life within the universe. Humanity is neither the center of the universe, nor its primary purpose. And while humans exist today, they have not always existed—nor will they always exist."

*****

I asked, "So, what are we supposed to do—I mean in terms of figuring out our role in the universe—our purpose, if you will, in life?"

Lee nodded. It seemed, for once, he thought my question wasn't stupid.

"Each woman, each man, must realize that their experience in the universe is a singular opportunity for self-definition. That means each human determines their own reason for being—their purpose in life. At birth, each person is given a context for their life—a period of history, individual strengths, weaknesses and an economic and social set of circumstances. Throughout their life, challenges and opportunities present themselves. Beyond those variables, each person owns their own experience. Regardless of whether she or he acknowledges that reality, each person owns the responses they make to the opportunities and challenges they face. In their response, each person defines their place in the universe. They end up making the universe a better place by increasing harmony; or they make it a worse place by reducing harmony."

In bringing up harmony, Lee had changed gears. He must have read my look because he responded as if I had just asked him what harmony meant.

62

"What is harmony? Harmony is constructive co-existence. Each element that someone touches represents an opportunity for harmony in the universe. There is an unimaginable number of living elements on the earth that are not human—animals, microorganisms, insects, birds, plants and so on. Individual elements coexist in the environments of rivers, oceans, lakes, soil, forests, air, and in other living bodies—and that speaks only to life on earth. A harmony in the universe is the constructive coexistence between any two or more elements or between elements and their environment."

His statement about harmony was so grand, it left me intellectually reeling.

He leaned his head to the side, looked at me and said, "You are already familiar with the concept of *harmony*. In music, individual sounds resonate with one another to create a whole sound that is more complete than the sum of the individual tones. That same principle can be applied to any circumstance where multiple pieces coexist and complement one another. Across the universe, the opportunities for harmony—or disharmony—are limitless. *Disharmony* is the lack of harmony—when sounds conflict with one another. The result of those discords is not pleasant to the ear."

Lee sighed. "Each person must define what harmony is—for themselves—then determine how they will achieve it. Until a person has determined how they are going to pursue harmony, that person will not be able to understand the underlying essence of the universe. Once a person ensconces themselves in the pursuit of harmony, she or he comes to understand intuitively what is beyond their capability of knowing intellectually. After that, a person can begin to perceive God as he or she comes to know the rhythm of their own personal universe."

Lee gave a friendly smile. "Let me tie today's lesson together. Questions about how and why the world was created are non-sensical. The world exists. The highest purpose in the universe—and thus of God—is the constant delivery of harmony. If a person wishes to understand God or the universe, that person must set aside primitive myths and go about their business of defining, exploring, and embracing their personal harmony."

He smiled at me and said, "Our time is up."

And with those words, Mr. Lee slowly stood up, bowed, and began to leave the room.

"Wait a second," I said. "You talk about harmony—but how about kindness, generosity, love, justice, and all the other values that I feel make human beings special? Isn't there a desire on your part to have people reach forward for those higher values?"

Mr. Lee sighed. "Human beings have a strong desire to define and codify ethics. But it seems that the same people who create ethical systems reward behaviors that conflict with those codes of ethics. Yes, your culture expresses belief in justice, love, humility, and generosity. But consider for a moment: Is there a preponderance of justice in your society—of love or humility or generosity in the day-to-day workings of your culture? I don't think so. Is there order? Yes. But is there harmony?"

He stood there, appearing to wait for a response. I chose not to give one.

Lee continued. "If a civilization decides to proclaim the harmonic social structures of justice, love, humility and generosity and those features become dominant in the society's day-to-day life, that would be good. But I don't see that too often. Civilizations do create order. But rarely do they achieve harmony. Harmony may have order, but order does not ensure harmony. Across the universe, the highest values coincide with harmony. If a human wishes to elevate herself or himself in the universe, she or he must come to visualize the harmony they seek—then pursue it. But if the result is values that are proclaimed, but not embraced in behavior; well, isn't that pretty empty?"

Again, I did not respond to the question. I waited.

"Human civilizations have created many wonderful ideals, but have achieved few of them. Much of the universe is in harmony—but human civilizations exist largely in conflict and humanity constantly suffers from disharmony. Humans suffer from hypocrisy— from the inability to embrace in their behavior the value structures they proclaim in their words. For humanity to live in balance with the universe, something different than greater verbal commitments is required."

Mr. Lee stood up, placed his palms together in a prayer-like manner, leaned his head forward toward me, and left the room

6: What is Life?

The next few evenings were dedicated to transcribing and studying Mr. Lee's comments. I kept asking myself how much of what he had said was meaningful and how much of it was just designed to distract. My conclusion was that most of what I'd heard in the first two meetings had been explanations of why my questions were invalid. I decided to employ a strategy for the coming session that would force more direct answers. I needed to be more aggressive.

*****

The following Sunday, as I sat in the lobby waiting for whoever the hell was going to show up, I focused on my strategy for avoiding being lectured on my ignorance. Time passed. As I waited, I became more frustrated with the entire process. I walked over to the conference room. No one was there. I checked it again five minutes later. It was still empty. I began to wonder if I had messed up on the meeting time or location. Or maybe Anderson, Elenore and Lee (it sounded like a law firm) were done with the show. At 11:30, I decided I had had it. I was going to forget about the whole thing and head home. My fantasy meetings with God were finished.

*****

As I emerged from the library and headed toward my car, an attractive black woman approached me. The woman's hair was in an afro and she was wearing tight blue jeans with a form-fitting, shape revealing, dark gray sweater.

67

She smiled at me, then said, "Call me Jessie. Last week, at the end of our get-together, you were feeling empty because I hadn't given you the simplistic answers you sought. Today, I wanted to let you wait a little—let your angst build up. We will begin today where we left off last week—you feeling empty and frustrated. But that is good, Joseph. Emptiness is the forerunner of understanding."

Jessie followed that by saying, "It's a nice day for a walk. Let's go."

After saying that she turned around and headed north. I was thinking maybe I should just forget about all this crap, get in my car and head home. But I didn't. Feeling a bit sheepish, I shrugged my shoulders and followed.

*****

After a few minutes walking in silence, Jessie started the day's discussion. "It isn't lost on me that your plan for today was to complain about how unresponsive I've been to your questions—how empty you felt at the end of our meeting. But as I said a moment ago, emptiness, Joseph, it's not a bad thing. Emptiness represents capacity. Emptiness is the tension that drives the universe. Thirst is the emptiness that causes one to drink. Hunger is the emptiness that makes one want to eat. Your frustration is the emptiness that precedes your learning. Your curiosity has been stimulated. Today, Joseph, curiosity did not kill the cat. Today, emptiness will open the door for the cat—in this case you—to learn something—

68

something new about the universe—to refresh your attitude toward life."

This was cute, but going nowhere. My aggravation must have been pretty obvious because Jessie shook her head and, after giving me a doubtful glance, said, "Come on, man. Chill out. Take a breath. You are alive. It's a beautiful day. We'll walk for a while. That should calm you down."

We continued down the street. As we walked, my tension slowly did diminish. Jessie had been right. I was calming down. We stopped for a moment in the middle of a block and watched a homeowner load a few pieces of broken-down furniture onto the back of an old Ford F-150. A minute later, when the homeowner got into the truck and moved on, so did we.

It took a few blocks before Jessie spoke again. "Like I said last week, most humans, including you, believe people are the most sophisticated form of life in the universe—of course other than their imaginary Gods. Humans believe that none of the animate objects around them are capable of conscious reasoning. If I were to say, *humans are correct in those beliefs*, would you feel better? Would your frustration end?"

I figured her question was rhetorical. I was right because Jessie paused for only a moment, then said, "If I said that to you, I'd only be encouraging your ignorance. From the outset, you've constantly worried that these interviews are just a hoax—that I am not God—that I am not being honest with you about anything. But Joseph, you are the one who is not being honest. You say you want the truth. But you get frustrated when I reject the unrealistic fantasies that are subtexts for each and every one of your questions. Whether you admit it or not, your real wish is for me to validate human fantasies in my responses. When that doesn't happen, you become frustrated. Isn't that sort of childish?"

I didn't respond. We continued to walk and there was no conversation a few minutes.

Then, Jessie said, "I have some sorry news for you, pal. If you're waiting for me to embrace that childlike view of the universe, we should say goodbye—here and now—call it a day. For us to make any progress, you're going to have to reject your naive paradigms. You're going to have to set aside your childish frustration and open up to some fresh perspectives."

It had been my plan to be the aggressor that day. I was going to take her—or whoever showed up—to task. But that certainly wasn't what had happened. Jessie had caught me off-guard. I wasn't sure what to say. So, I said nothing. We just walked. Her words gradually stopped stinging and began to soak in.

Jessie broke the silence. "Sorry. But I had to start out by calling you out. It avoided you making a bigger fool of yourself by accusing me of being a fraud."

She laughed.

I didn't.

*****

We walked without any further interchange for ten minutes. It was a cool, sunny, spring day. I began to enjoy the walk. After a while, I stopped strategizing about how to deal with her. I began to relax. We arrived at a small park that overlooked a stunning view of Puget Sound and the Olympic Mountains. Jessie sat down on a park bench and gestured for me to sit next to her. I sat down, pulled out my pen and pad from my small backpack and began to write. Jessie waited while I jotted down the things that had already been said. When I looked up, ready to continue, Jessie was looking out at the view of Puget Sound. I did the same.

She took a deep breath, let it out slowly, and said, "Today, we're discussing the question, W*hat is life*? I'm gonna start out again by asking you if I should begin with a parable or a definition."

Each week, she had spoken about whether she should start out with a metaphor, some sort of simple explanation or both. Then she would lecture about human beings' misinterpretations of metaphors. I wanted to avoid that lecture and said in a sort of sarcastic manner, "Go ahead, Jessie. Give me the truth—as best I can understand it. What is life? And, if you would, please explain how I fit into the universe."

Before she could respond, I added, "I heard a joke—years ago—that sort of summarizes my request. I'm sure you're familiar with the story of Adam and Eve."

Jessie smirked and said, "Yeah. I think I've heard that one a couple of times. That was a hell of a metaphor—wasn't it? But man, did it ever get way out of control."

"Well," I said, "this version of the story goes like this. God created Adam and Eve. The couple looked around at the Garden of Eden in wonder. Suddenly Eve got this puzzled look on her face. God noticed it and said, *What's wrong Eve?* Eve says to God, *Now, what do we do?* Well, God shook his head and said, *I don't know, Eve—that's your problem.*"

Jessie chuckled. I'd always thought that that was a pretty good joke and was pleased she enjoyed it as well.

I continued. "Even though it's a joke, Jessie, it addresses—head on—what I'm asking you today." I thought about it for a moment and added, "Maybe it's what I've been asking from the outset. When I say *what is life*, I am really asking what are humans? How do we fit into this world? Where did we come from? Where are we going?"

Jessie nodded. "Thank you, Joseph. That was well said—and an excellent start for today's discussion. I'll speak about your theme for the week and then move into those related questions. So, what is life? It is inner-driven movement and all other activity not driven only by inertia. Life is active pursuit of fulfillment within and between planes in the universe. Life includes both a capacity to move and the drive to direct that motion."

She waited while I jotted down that definition.

"That's interesting," I said. "But it's a lot to absorb in just a few words. I'm going to have to take some time during the coming week to go through it. Go ahead with your—uhm—your *lecture*."

I laughed first. She joined in.

"Much of the constant activity that defines the universe is created by life. Life is intentional movement—not simply a display of momentum. To illustrate, the orbit of the earth around the sun or the movement of light from a star are examples of momentum. Life is intentional actions from, between and among living things as well as intentional and involuntary reactions to other activity in the universe."

Jessie had begun to speak slowly. "The size of the universe," she said, "is so much grander than anything you can begin to imagine. And the number of lives in the universe corresponds directly to that size. The universe—life—is the infinity that encompasses you."

Jessie stood up and walked toward the edge of the park to a chain link fence that overlooked Puget Sound. I followed her and sat on a bench next to the fence so I could continue to take notes. We looked out across the sea towards the Olympic Mountains. The only sound I heard came from sea gulls calling out to one another in the distance.

Her voice became gentler as she continued to speak at a slow pace. "You are comfortable with my using the term *infinity*. But my using that word in describing the universe and the lives within it is problematic. Humans feel comfortable using that term because it allows them to speak about something they cannot comprehend as if they understood it. But the term *infinity* requires more than a definition. The universe including the breadth of life within it goes beyond anything you can even begin to comprehend. Accepting that reality requires humility."

Jessie gazed across the horizon and inhaled deeply. After she exhaled, she turned to me and said, "So it would be more meaningful for you if I describe life and the universe without using the word *infinity*. The universe is dynamic, layered, multi-dimensional and unending. The universe includes many realms you are aware of and countless others that are beyond what you are able to perceive."

She paused again. This time, it wasn't for me to catch up in my notes. I think she intended to give me a moment to consider the magnitude of what she had just said.

Jessie said, "OK?"

I nodded.

She continued. "And for each and every living thing in the universe, there are multiple levels of life—above, below and around. Your body is made up of multiple levels of other living elements and systems. You know this. But you do not know the complexity of those lives. Many earth species live around you. Each of them is also at the top of a living pyramid. You are also, of course, a component of multiple systems—of families, of tribes and of the human race."

I just replied, "OK. I get that."

She smiled. "You are aware of your own conscious experience. But you—and most other humans—believe that other types and levels of elements—down the chain and around you—are without a conscious awareness. That belief is incorrect. It ignores the countless other types of life that exist on your planet and across the universe—some you are aware of and many others of which you are not—some you cannot even begin to imagine. Each life is a part of complex systems and a host for others."

I understood what she had said. If this was true, it was mindboggling. I continued with my notes, figuring I would have to wrestle with the implications of what she had said later in the week.

*****

At that point, I changed the subject. "Jessie, what about death? What happens to a person when they die? You say that physical and psychic phenomena are different aspects of the same things. Does that mean, that when a body dies, as in *dust to dust*, that a person's psychic qualities, their so-called soul, also ends? If that is true, you wouldn't just be telling me there is no boat to the Field of Reeds or heaven—you would be saying that when a person dies, that's it—the end. No ghosts; no after-life; no nothing.

"Appropriate question," she said. "But a tough and complex question. One of the most difficult parts of trying to describe what is beyond your experience is that metaphors and definitions have their limits. In addition, humans tend to focus on whatever might follow their current life experience. But that is a mistake. They own their current experience."

Jessie sat down next to me. A moment later, she smiled and said, "Why don't we approach your inquiry by borrowing from some of my other statements? You recall when I said the universe is multi-dimensional—that it includes large realms that are beyond your ability to perceive?"

I nodded again.

"Well," she said, "you have identified such a realm here. The consciousness that many humans refer to as your soul, that other people refer to as psychic energies or karma, combines with and responds to other similar vitalities in the universe. Each person's consciousness retains some of integrity while integrating with other energies. It is complex and takes place in dimensions and ways that are beyond anything you can perceive or comprehend. I would be foolish to try to simplify those dimensions with a metaphor or a definition or worse yet, a story with a moral. I've tried that. It didn't work. Talk about giving ammunition for future misunderstandings!"

She gave a large sigh and said, "Suffice it to say that the way of the world is the pursuit of harmony and that those energies are an element in that dynamic. But I should repeat my caution that the effort to create harmony for each being—not just for humans—should focus on their current experience. Let the other dimensions take care of themselves."

Joseph Imagines God

Jessie said nothing for several minutes. She just looked out across Puget Sound. After a while, she leaned her head to the side and said, "All of the elements within the universe feed into this stream of life—like creeks feeding into a river. But unlike a river, the flow is up, down, inside, outside, across, forward and backward. Elements constantly feed off of other elements' energy—constantly work together—or against one another. That conflict and adhesion defines life. The rhythms and the harmonics—the order within and between these tensions—create the magic that causes humans to believe there is a plan—that the world is not chaos—that there must be a God. But, as I said before, God is not separate from these elements— not above them; God is the fundamental unifying quality within the cosmos."

A bald eagle soared above us—chased by a crow. We both watched the eagle and the crow for a moment. Jessie was still watching these birds as she said, "So, what is the relationship between individual lives and the universe? Many elements constantly striving to survive and find harmony within a great and elegant construct."

I looked up after writing down her last statement. Jessie was silent again, gazing out across Puget Sound. A fresh breeze was blowing towards us. I inhaled the clean air—then let it out slowly. A cloud sailed silently above us. Other clouds below it remained stationary. Seagulls were gliding, circling, and calling out to one another. The bald eagle soared past us again; then dipped toward the waters of Puget Sound. We watched this extraordinary show for several minutes.

"Consciousness," Jessie said while continuing to look across the Sound, "defining who you are—requires you to focus on what you are able to perceive—and also upon what you can imagine. So, in a sense, Joseph, you are the center of your universe. But always remember, that every element that lives is at the center of its own universe. Your objective must be to take all that is around you seriously; yet never treat yourself too seriously. Your actions define you. The bigness, the impenetrability of this world should not threaten you as you seek to find peace within it. Instead, it should encourage you to remain humble."

She turned to me with an intense gaze. "Humans need to spend less time worrying about their own significance in the universe. They need to spend more time listening to and considering how their behavior impacts the rhythms and harmonies around them."

*****

After Jessie finished saying that, she returned her attention to the view of Puget Sound and the Olympic Mountains. A moment later, she stood up, said, "It has been very pleasant, Joseph. I will see you next week."

And she walked away.

As I walked back to my car and later, as I drove home, I felt good. In spite of the fact that my intent for the day had been to demand specific answers which were not given, I was at peace. I had begun to understand why I hadn't gotten the answers for which I had hoped.

Or maybe better said, I was in harmony with what Jessie had said.

7: What is the Value of Religion?

I was wondering what the next *God* would look like as I sat waiting in the library lobby the following Sunday morning. The entrance door swung open and my wife walked into the lobby. My heart sunk. This was going to be difficult. During the preceding week, she had asked me more than once about what she referred to as my *mysterious Sunday trips to the library*. I told her I was doing research for a project—which was more or less true.

My wife surveyed the lobby for a moment, spotted me, gave a smile and walked over. Why she was there? Was she delivering a message—perhaps an emergency at work? But if that was the case, why hadn't she just called me on my cell? Did her arrival mean that whoever was playing God that day would stay away—or, worse yet, would they have to explain what was going on to my wife? Or had my wife decided I'd been lying about my trips to the library? This was awful!

As she approached, with a smirk on her face, I panicked. I tried to keep my face calm as I labored over what to say. Should I introduce her to whomever was pretending to be God? But I had no idea what that person would look like and I'd promised not to tell anyone about our meetings.

I was flummoxed.

*****

Calmly, my wife said, "You can relax, Joseph. I'm not your wife. I've come in her persona because the

80

library staff have been gossiping about our weekly meetings. Librarians always have been nosy and this crew is particularly curious. Playing your wife today was the obvious solution—don't you agree?"

She laughed. I didn't.

Then she added, "And on top of that, I wanted to see your face when I arrived. The look you gave did not disappoint."

*****

She looked, acted and sounded like my wife. Suddenly, it hit me like a ton of bricks. My wife was in on the conspiracy. She had been sharing my notes with the others while I was at work. That explained a whole lot of things—but why did she do it?

I wondered if I should call her on it, then and there. But I wasn't certain enough that it was my wife—though it really did look like her. And I couldn't believe she would participate in that sort of prank. So, I chose the path of a coward. I ignored the bizarre circumstances. But what if this wasn't my wife and my real wife walked in on the conversation? What would happen then?

My wife—God or whomever it was—looked at me curiously and said, "I see you're worrying. I understand why. Those worries are unnecessary. Your wife will not walk in on our meeting. No one will say they saw her here today. Next week, we will meet somewhere else. But today, let's get out of here. Let's go for a drive—say to Warm Beach. We can talk on the way and when we get there, we'll be able to enjoy a nice stroll along the beach."

When I hesitated, she laughed and added, "You drive, Joseph. I don't believe I have a current Washington State license."

I shook my head, then joined her in laughter. This was getting curiouser and curiouser.

*****

Ten minutes later, we were on our way, driving toward Interstate 5. I turned to her and said, "You look like my wife. I am not going to call you God—and I don't feel comfortable calling you by her name. What should I call you?"

"Oh," she responded with an almost flirtatious smile, "You can call me Delilah. But don't worry, I promise not to cut your hair."

She repeated the flirtatious smile and added, "But, Joseph, you really do need a haircut."

I took a deep breath before responding. My wife would have said the same thing in the same tone.

"OK, Delilah," I said. "It's going to take us most of an hour to get there. When I left home, I told my wife—uhm—you know, the real one—that I would be back by 12:30. There is no way...."

Delilah interrupted my stammered statement. "Take a deep breath, Joe. Everything is going to be alright. Your wife will not be upset. I promise."

What could I say? I turned onto I-5 heading north.

Nothing was said for a quarter of an hour. When I turned off of the interstate onto the Tulalips Indian Reservation where Warm Beach is located, Delilah turned to me and asked, "OK if we start?"

I was a little vexed at how this was going. I asked, "How am I supposed to take notes while I'm driving?"

She chuckled, rolled her eyes (exactly as my wife would have done) and said, "Relax Joseph. When you sit down later this week to transcribe this conversation, you will have a clear memory of everything that was said. Trust me—and relax."

I didn't respond. What ran through my mind was that my only choices were to cooperate with Delilah or to turn the car around and head back to town.

*****

Delilah jumped into a lecture. "You've given me another straightforward question: *What is the value of religion?* However, once again, I'm afraid my answer will not meet your expectations."

She had anticipated the topic one more time and I wasn't surprised at all that she said she was not going to give me a response that I expected.

"How you describe existing religions," she began, "is going to be of interest to anyone who reads your document about these meetings. You need to be clear from the outset—religion is not about God. Religion is about people—their fears, their needs and their social structures. God—and listen closely on this—has rarely been accurately described by a religion. Religions may be the primary path people use to reach out to God, but they often are the primary reason people don't have any understanding of God."

*****

I reflected on how hard it would be for anyone to believe what I am describing. But let me assure you, it was even stranger to experience. Delilah, in every respect, looked like my wife. Every nuance of how she spoke sounded like my wife. Her mannerisms mirrored those of my wife. But the intense theoretical focus she brought to her presentation that Sunday—well, as I sat listening to her—I became certain I was not listening to my wife.

*****

"Human beings are social animals," she said. "They form alliances or tribes to achieve common objectives. Going back tens of thousands of years, humans have depended upon tribes for survival. In primitive times, tribal members protected one another from threats and worked together to secure food and shelter. But tribes also have been—and still are—the fundamental social fabric of humanity."

As we drove toward Warm Beach, I saw a large animal on the road a couple of hundred yards ahead of us. Delilah also saw it and stopped speaking. I slowed, then stopped the car. Standing in front of us in the middle of the roadway was a magnificent stag. The large deer had walked halfway across the road before stopping. It stood calmly in the middle of the road, head and multi-pointed antlers turned toward us. We watched him and he watched us. After a couple of minutes, the large buck slowly looked away from us toward the other side the road, then gracefully finished his crossing. After he melted into the woods, I put the car back into drive and we continued on our way toward Warm Beach.

Delilah was silent for a couple more minutes. When she did speak, she returned to her lecture as if there hadn't been an interruption. "Let's start out by distinguishing between a religion and a religious sanctuary. A religion is a set of beliefs about God, humans and the universe. But it is also a bureaucracy—sometimes a huge bureaucracy. The sanctuary, under the leadership of one or more priests, hosts formal religious ceremonies and social events. It is also the base from which support is offered to members of the faith during hard times."

It seemed like Delilah was approaching this discussion in an almost academic manner. In fact, each week she—or he—had begun her analysis with contexts and definitions. Her logical thoroughness would have made her an excellent budget analyst. I almost made a wisecrack, asking her if I could hire her to join our county government's budget team. But I decided such a joke would seem like a stupid comment at best—and an insult at worst. So, I just forgot about telling my joke and continued to listen.

The moment I decided not to tell the joke, Delilah gave me an odd look, shook her head, and chuckled. My wife would have responded to one of my dumb jokes in exactly the same manner.

Delilah continued. "A religion is a tribe that offers rules to guide members' lives and gives them myths that demystify the universe. Those myths are the cornerstone of the religion's authority in that they serve as a record of the religion's alliance with God or gods. They also lay out certain moral and behavioral expectations."

*****

Delilah paused. We slowed down as we passed a small white Honda Civic. A tribal police officer was giving a traffic ticket to a young blonde woman who appeared to be crying. I decided I better be careful not to speed. The last thing I needed was to have some cop stop us and ask Delilah for a piece of identification.

*****

Once we passed the Civic, Delilah returned to her lecture. "Modern civilization still depends on tribes. Those tribes have evolved from the primitive structures of the past. In fact, you don't even call them tribes any more. Modern people are too sophisticated to refer to their organizations as tribes. But tribes they are. Modern tribes have retained the same purposes as tribes have embodied for millennia—the safety, economic and social well-being of their members."

Delilah leaned back in her seat and looked out her side window while saying to me, "You belong to many tribes, Joe. The employees at work are a tribe. Your high school and college are tribes that shaped you when you were young. Your health club and food co-op are smaller, but useful tribes. And you, Joseph—you are an American! That's a big powerful tribe. And, as in ancient times, religious organizations are important tribes that wield enormous amounts of power."

It was turning into a bright sunny day. Delilah opened her small *Coach* shoulder bag. She reached into it and pulled out a pair of sunglasses. The dark navy-blue shoulder bag and the tortoise shell framed sunglasses were identical to my wife's.

Once Delilah had put on her sunglasses, she continued. "Religions often provide a wonderful service to their communities. When a person is afraid, when she or he despairs or suffers, or when someone is overwhelmed by the hardness of the world, a religion can make a huge difference. A sanctuary's leaders and members can help that person find peace—identify solutions. The simplicity of a quiet place of worship can turn into the most wonderful location in the world for a person in distress. Praying in silence can allow harmony for someone who has been overcome by the disharmony around them."

Delilah paused, letting that sink in. Then she said, "Religious leaders should not simply recite a series of incantations, rules or myths—words that can totally ignore the chaos in their parishioners' lives. The religious leader must have compassion when listening to members who face tragedy. They must be able to respond from the heart. He or she must accept that the troubled person standing in front of them is often facing challenges that go well beyond the leader's personal experience. A religious leader who has wisdom, compassion and insight has the tools to help a troubled person cope with extreme adversity," Delilah hesitated before adding, "if that religious leader retains humility."

Her voice changed as she said, "But I know that my description of how a religious leader should behave is often not how they act. I know that priests and religious leaders often fail to meet the promises they make. I would be dishonest if I didn't admit that religions and their leaders often end up doing much more harm than good."

Delilah stopped speaking as we turned off of the two-lane highway onto the access road that would take us to Warm Beach. A few minutes later, after I parked my car, we walked toward the beach.

*****

About a hundred feet from the water, Delilah sat down on a great log and stretched her legs. She looked out across Puget Sound, smiled and inhaled deeply.

After exhaling, she said, "I assume you want to know what I think of each religion—today and in the past?"

I didn't respond.

She chuckled before saying, "There have been a lot of religions and while the rules of each one was created in the name of a God or of Gods, the rules of one religion often are in direct conflict with the rules of other faiths. Many religions teach that their rules and beliefs are the only true set—almost as if their religion's founders had some sort of special knowledge about the universe. Of course, some religions actually claim that God instructed their leaders to set up the faith. But I can tell you, I was not a party to those conversations. And memorizing and obeying a complex religious doctrine will never lead to any sort of salvation."

She looked out across the water. I followed her gaze and saw a cormorant swoop down, diving into the waves of Puget Sound. Moments later, the bird came to the surface holding some sort of small fish in its bill.

Delilah looked back at me and said, "You want to know if religion can make humanity's world worse? Joseph, you know the answer to that one. All you had to do was read a little bit of world history and consider some of the so-called holy wars that have been waged throughout human history—and are still happening today."

She sighed and said, "Many religious movements have aggressively created disharmony. Religions formed partnerships with governments that oppressed people. They sponsored or endorsed the slaughter and oppression of members of weaker tribes. They blessed causes that ended up in rape, murder and dehumanization while land and wealth were stolen from innocent victims. This was done—in the name of the Lord. And it continues to this day."

Delilah stopped speaking. She had an intense look on her face.

"Not all of their evil deeds are so obvious," she said in a grim tone. "Some religions encourage their members to mistreat those who practice other faiths. Faiths openly or tacitly condone efforts to exclude, degrade or mistreat those who have different colors of skin; who speak another language; or happen to love members of their own sex. It amazes me, Joseph, how much cruelty has been perpetrated in this world by self-righteous people who proclaim that they are my representatives. They say they speak about love. They promise peace. But what they promote amounts to cruelty and violence."

My wife is a gentle, positive person. She appreciates and focuses upon details rather than philosophical judgments. Delilah's last statements were delivered with a severity that was akin to anger. This definitely was not my wife.

Delilah stood up and walked toward the surf. I followed. She picked up a stone and skipped it across the water. It was quite a throw. The stone skipped off of the water at least ten times before disappearing into the sea. That throw confirmed, once again, that this wasn't my wife. If my wife had tossed a stone across the water, it would have immediately disappeared into the sea.

*****

I decided to ask Delilah why she continually criticized myths, then often used stories to illustrate her points. But before I could begin to ask that, she responded to my still unspoken question.

"I guess," she said, "it would be useful for me to explain how metaphors, parables and allegories—the illustrations I use so often—are different from myths. In previous sessions, I have spoken about the value of stories as a means of describing something to humans that is beyond their experience. I used the example of Plato's allegory of the cave. Now, you are confused because I have been criticizing myths. You must wonder what the difference is between my illustrations and a myth?"

As she moved from one idea to the next, Delilah's lecture style reminded me of Dr. Iseminger, my college Introduction to Philosophy teacher. "A myth adds detail to the story of a metaphor, parable or allegory. It makes the fictional story seem like a historical event while often losing its underlying meaning."

She looked at me, perhaps to see if I was tracking with her comments. I was a little confused by her last statement and she must have figured that out because she added to it.

"For example," she said. "To turn the allegory of Plato's cave into a myth, one would simply add a bunch of details. The central character would be given a name and developed into a hero, a fool, or a victim full of strengths or weaknesses. He would either rise above the limited amount of available information about the world or suffer some sort of misery for lack of that information. More details about the cave or other characters would also be added to the story."

91

Delilah picked up a small stone and threw it into the sea. After a moment, she said, "The downside? Well, the story might have been more enjoyable to listen to, but its meaning would be lost. If turned into a myth, the value of Plato's cave allegory would most likely become a distant echo of what it is as an allegory. It would lose its point—that humans live in a world beyond their conscious comprehension."

During our time at Warm Beach, several more questions occurred to me. But in each instance, Delilah was able to anticipate my question. As our walk progressed, it became obvious to me that I should relax—just absorb rhythm of her words—and her wisdom.

*****

She picked up another stone and threw it far from the shore. Then she turned back to me and said, "I spoke to you about the Christian myth that was driven by a metaphor of innocence and vulnerability— qualities that the original metaphor proclaimed most dear to God—you know the story—the one about the baby who was born into absolute poverty in a farm shed before being honored by kings. Well, in modern times, this myth is celebrated with a display— oftentimes a shed that is occupied by figurines of humans and barn animals. Each December, sheds like this are placed next to churches—churches that cost millions of dollars to build. If a poor homeless man sought shelter in one of these sheds, he would be arrested for public vagrancy. That is an excellent example of a metaphor which lost its meaning after it became a myth."

Delilah went on, "Another method of illustration that is used to teach is through kōans."

I responded, "I'm not familiar with kōans."

Delilah said, "Kōans are brief stories or riddles that lead to a question rather than a conclusion. A kōan is the opposite of a myth. It pushes a person to think beyond the boundaries of traditional logic rather than leading them to a pat conclusion. A kōan challenges an individual to respond to a question that seems to have no logical answer. Zen Buddhists use kōans to approach the unknown—to expand their capability to accept the fullness of the world."

*****

Delilah turned and walked along the beach. I followed.

"Religions," she said, "create standards of behavior and prescribe sets of beliefs for their members to embrace in their lives. Sometimes, these standards are values that provide guidance in navigating the complexities of life. But often, they are better described as rules. Followers are expected to obey these rules rather than take personal responsibility in determining how they should behave. These rules can result in a sort of ethical passiveness— a type of moral fatalism. You know, *I live this way because God wants me to.*"

Delilah interrupted her speech for a few moments as we watched a sailboat slice its way across the Puget Sound waters. As the boat came about, I reflected upon what she had said. Her words seemed to be full of truth.

Delilah looked away from the sailboat, turned toward me and said, "So why does a religion's membership trust their religious leaders and follow their decrees? Myths are a mechanism for legitimizing religious authority. Devotees do not question the license that myths seem to bestow upon a religion and its leaders because those myths ostensibly reflect the will of God."

We started walking down the beach. She added, "This does not mean that all religious rules are without value. But an autocratic method of enforcing behavior eliminates the growth that occurs when a person's struggles to discover their own moral truth. And sadly," Delilah looked down and slowly shook her head, "the rules promoted under the authority of these myths are often devoid of wisdom."

*****

"I get it." I told her, "You're saying religions use myths as the proof that their message is righteous— that they speak for God. A religion's leaders can tell their followers what is right and what is wrong—as if it were the will of God."

"Yes, they do," Delilah said. "And those rules and judgements often are questionable. In Hinduism, lower castes have been taught to strictly adhere to rules that limit them in this life in the hope that they can move to a higher caste in the next. Leaders of almost every religion endorse corrupt wars and vilify individuals who challenge those wars' moral basis. Interfaith marriages are prohibited in countless faiths without regard to the love of those who desire to marry. Jewish leaders condone Israeli discrimination against Palestinians. Christian leaders judge those who choose to have abortions. There is an endless list of instances where religious laws are cruel *and* self-righteous."

We walked for a while. I thought that maybe she was done with reciting the faults of religions. I was wrong.

"Religions—in the name of God—have caused entire communities to ignore catastrophic problems. When the ancient Greeks suffered from illness or drought, their priests often told them that the Gods were angry and the drought or illness was a punishment. The priests told those who would listen that the Gods could be appeased with animal sacrifices. The sacrifices were made. They may not have improved conditions, but they allowed spiritual followers to believe they were addressing the catastrophe. What do you think, Joseph? Do you believe that there might have been a more effective way of responding to illness or drought than killing livestock who were needed for the people's sustenance?"

I was about to respond to her rhetorical question when she said, "But it gets worse. When the Ancient Mayans suffered from famine, their priests told them it was because the Mayan God Chaac was angry. The priests explained that Chaac could be appeased by the ritual murder of young boys. So, in heavily stylized rituals, boys' heads were cut off and their hearts removed. Mayan tribal members felt they had done what was necessary, that Chaac would be appeased. But I doubt their sacrifice made sense to the young boys who were murdered—and it certainly didn't bring any rain. Do you think it made sense?"

I did not attempt to respond to her rhetorical question. I just waited.

"These Greek and Mayan priests told their followers what had caused their suffering and then committed a violent act—ostensibly to diminish suffering in an otherwise uncertain world. Community members felt safer—but the community took no other actions to end the suffering. These violent deeds in the name of God accomplished nothing and resulted in communities not dealing with a disaster."

We walked without words for a few minutes before she said in a sad voice, "There are countless examples of religions encouraging their members to behave in ways that decrease harmony. Examples include the exclusion of people who love people of their own sex from tribal membership or leadership; offering parallel education systems to people of different ethnic or racial backgrounds as a means of avoiding integration; and not allowing girls to attend school. The days of sacrificing children at an alter may have passed, but in some parts of the world, a bomb is attached to a child's body and the child is used as a weapon—with a promise to the child that he or she will be rewarded for her or his heroism in the next life."

*****

Delilah anticipated my next question. "You want to know if the stories in the Torah, the New Testament, the Qur'an, the Śruti texts and the Tipiṭaka offer truth? Yes, they do—but don't take them too literally. While these books carry truth, they are not histories and should definitely not be treated as a set of rules. They are designed to teach. They invite interpretation. Each statement in these books has many valid interpretations—some of which are contradictory. Those who claim to know with certainty which interpretation is correct and which is invalid are fools, liars or just plain naive."

After saying this, Delilah stopped walking. She sat down on a log, took off her shoes and rolled her jeans up to her knees. Then she stood up, shoes in hand and waded into the shallow cold surf. She looked back at me over her shoulder and said, "C'mon. You should try this."

Figuring, what the hell, I sat down on the log, pulled off my socks and tennis shoes, rolled up my blue jeans and followed her into the water. Moments later, I was standing next to Delilah in the surf. The cold clear water was exhilarating.

*****

Delilah turned to me and said, "Now, I am going to ask you a question. Do you think religion can bring a person closer to God?"

I was caught off guard, but decided this question was not rhetorical. I answered, "Yes. Probably. But I am here to listen to you. You tell me."

She smiled—it was a warm smile—and said, "Yes, religion can bring people closer to God. It can happen when religious leaders teach their members to embrace harmony. However, it is not accomplished by promoting a gauntlet of myths or by establishing repressive, constrictive rules."

We continued to walk through the surf. I appreciated the sound of seawater rushing onto the beach and the quiet as it streamed back into Puget Sound.

Delilah said, "One more question: How do you think a priest teaches harmony?"

This was a tougher question. I decided to wait and let her answer her own question.

After a couple minutes when she didn't answer the question, I gave it a shot. "A priest can teach harmony by encouraging a church member not to be reactive; by urging them to be patient in their quest for understanding. The priest should encourage their members to have inner dialogues—internal conversations full of honesty."

Delilah laughed and exclaimed, "Wow! Pretty damn wise for an accountant."

I joined her in laughter.

Then she added, "The religious elder should preach humility and compassion rather than arrogance and dogma. He or she must advise that once a person has figured out the right thing to do, they must act upon that recognition. Knowledge without follow through is an empty vessel. In a nutshell, the religious leader should try to help their parishioner find wisdom—then encourage them to have the faith to act on it. And those priests need to teach their congregations that wisdom is a product of meditation—peaceful watching, listening and contemplation. And they must explain that in order to become wise, one must be humble."

We left the surf and returned to the sandy beach. Sitting on another massive log, we put on our shoes and socks, then continued our walk. I enjoyed our leisurely pace along the beach, listening to Delilah while not having to take notes. At one point, it occurred to me that even if this was some sort of a hoax, I didn't care. There seemed to be a lot of value in her words.

*****

"Anyway," Delilah continued, "a religion's leadership is the key. It isn't so much that certain religions are good or bad—although clearly some religions are not prone to encouraging meditation or wisdom. But when a religion is good, it's because its places of worship have good leaders. Unfortunately, many religious leaders—both priests and others from the community—are ambitious, self-righteous, self-centered fools."

"What do you really think," I wisecracked.

99

She smiled softly and said, "Ignorant and ambitious people sometimes see religious posts as paths to prestige—to places of power over other people. Those ambitious sorts find satisfaction in holding and exercising power. When a religion is led by such a person, the religious community is repressed—harmony recedes. On the other hand, when a religion, its teachers and its leaders, embrace and teach wisdom and humility, harmony grows. The community benefits."

Delilah was looking down at the sand and stones as she walked. She seemed almost sad and again shook her head slowly from side to side before saying, "Modern humans are often lonely and isolated. The cultural mechanisms of modern times—televisions and computers—are tools that create human isolation. Technology rarely leads to wisdom. It turns communities into economic market places rather than places where community members work together becoming partners in pursuit of harmony."

She stopped for a moment, looked out across the water. "Your schools often teach children to compete with one another rather than to work together. There is insufficient emphasis on trying to understand fellow students. That creates confusion for young members of your communities. Unfortunately, family members often lack the skills to respond properly when that occurs. Parents and children become isolated from one another."

Delilah looked directly at me and said, "Yes, Joseph. Religious groups can be a mechanism that takes all of this on. They can bring people together—and I know—humanity needs the help! A culture can heal when the tone of a religious group is positive, when its leaders create a fabric of trust and respect. Religious groups have the capacity to mitigate the isolation and competition that is so prevalent throughout much of your modern world. When that happens, a religion—a church—offers a pathway to harmony."

She gave me a warm smile. Yes, she looked like my wife. But her smile was different than my wife's. It wasn't less warm. It was just different—distant.

"I am glad," she said, "that you asked me about religion. Even though I do not depend upon religion to communicate with humans, religions can help humans relate to the universe—and within that context, help their members discover God. But the operative word in that sentence is *can.*"

Then she gave me a hug. I was embarrassed, unsure of why she gave me the hug.

I told her, "I am glad we came to the beach. It's beautiful here."

She said, "Yes, it is."

We turned around and quietly walked back along the path we had taken minutes before. I watched waves rolling up, then down, over the rocky beach. It had been a pleasant afternoon. Delilah's lecture had made sense. I turned toward her and suggested it was time to finish up.

Delilah said, "Yes, it is. Let's meet at Paesano's Coffee Shop on Colby next Sunday at eleven."

I was a little confused and said, "Don't you need a ride back to the library?"

She laughed and said, "I don't think that'll be required."

*****

I returned to my car and drove home. An hour later, I entered my home and called out to my wife.

At first there was no answer. A moment later, my wife came down the stairs.

"I'm sorry honey," she said. "After you took off for the library, I laid down to rest—just for a few minutes. But I fell asleep. And God, did I ever sleep deeply!"

She gave me a quick kiss and asked, "Did things go well at the library?"

I replied, "Yes, they did. But it's good to be home on such a beautiful day. We should go out and garden."

We enjoyed the rest of that sunny Sunday afternoon—weeding, fertilizing, tilling and pruning in our flower beds. As I finished up cultivating around a fragrant rosebush in full bloom, I realized it didn't make any difference whether this whole set of meetings was a hoax, whether I was nuts or whether I really was meeting with some sort of God.

I was learning.

8: How did God Communicate in the Past?

Over the next couple of days, I documented my meeting with Delilah. I was relieved that, as she had promised, I could recollect her lecture almost word for word.

*****

The week passed quickly. Soon it was Sunday—raining once again. I drove to the Paesano's on Colby Avenue for my meeting with...well, with whomever met me there. I arrived five minutes early and ordered a short coffee latte. From my seat at a corner table, I could look out the Paesano's storefront window and observed the café's entrance. As I sipped my latte, I inspected each person who passed Paesano's, trying to guess who would enter, approach me and become my next apparition of God.

An older black woman entered the coffee shop. She had a cane and walked with a pronounced limp. I figured she was the one. But after she bought a cup of drip coffee, she left the shop. A moment later, a young woman with pink and blue streaked hair entered the coffee shop. She walked straight towards me, stopped, seemed ready to say something, then pivoted and found a table on the other side of the café. Next was a young priest who shook the rain off of his green umbrella and looked directly at me. I waited for him to start a conversation, but he turned away, walked over and joined the young woman with the pink and blue streaks in her hair.

I was half-way done with my latte when the barista who was cleaning up a nearby table asked, "Can I take your cup?"

I told him, "No. I'm not finished."

The barista said, "Excuse me sir but I must ask, why are you here?"

I figured someone had complained that I had been eyeing his customers—probably the young woman with the pink and blue streaked hair. I told him, "I purchased a latte and am waiting for someone to join me. Is that a crime?"

The barista laughed, said, "Not today. Today you can call me Aaron"

He sat down at my table and moved right into a lecture. "So—you want to know about my conversations with other humans. Do you want me to begin with conversations from the past?" He snickered, before adding, "or would you like me to begin by telling you about conversations in the future?"

I just sighed and said, "Do your thing."

*****

It was clear by now, that whoever played God each week would know my question. I have since wondered if he or she knew the questions before I did. Was it possible he—or she—willed me to ask those specific questions? And as far as Aaron asking if I wanted to know about conversations with humans in the future, I wasn't even going to try to make a joke out of that one. I had already been told that I had no concept of time. I did not want to listen to another lecture on that. I just sat there and said nothing.

Aaron moved right into it. "You still don't have a clue what's going on between us, do you, Joseph? You keep wondering if you're imagining this whole thing or whether a group of your friends are having a lot of fun at your expense. You wonder whether you've been hypnotized or are losing your mind? And every now and then, you ask yourself if it's possible you are speaking with God. Then, a moment later, you wonder if I'm the devil." He laughed and said, "But you shouldn't feel so bad. Most of those to whom I've spoken have had similar fears."

I took out my notebook, sighed, and began to write.

He moved into the subject. "There is no standard approach for how I communicate, when I communicate, or to whom I communicate. Human beings receive input from me in different ways. Many of those who are in touch with the universe hear my message without any inkling that God has inspired them. Sometimes, the message is received through their intuition. Other times the path can be through their imagination, their inspirations, or their dreams."

"On the other hand," he said as he chuckled, "those who proclaim with the highest level of self-assurance that a divine intervention has taken place—that I have spoken to them—have either fabricated their whole stories or so misunderstood my message that their words carry more harm than good. If they had heard me clearly, they would be less arrogant in their demeanor. My communication with people has certainly not been limited to what's been recounted in holy books. And, no surprise, only some of those stories or ideas that are in the holy books were actually initiated by me."

He paused, looking around the café, and added, "I mustn't forget to mention the outright fraudsters— the self-righteous charlatans who claim that God regularly communicates with them. They construct ostentatious sanctuaries and constantly ask their flock for more money. Their messages are dishonest garbage."

*****

Aaron looked down at the empty cups, crumpled napkins and used plates he had collected from other tables before joining me. "Speaking of garbage," he said, "I have to dispose of this stuff. While I'm up, can I get you a chai latte?"

I laughed and said *yes,* amused at the absurdity of the circumstance.

Aaron returned to the service counter where he chatted briefly with the young woman who was now operating the store by herself. At the end of their brief dialog, she smiled and nodded. Aaron grabbed a cup, went behind the counter and soon was fixing a hot drink.

A few minutes later he returned to the table and handed me an excellent chai latte.

I picked up where he had left off moments before. "You're telling me there were false prophets—ones who invented their own messages? How can I tell which prophets were real?"

"You want me to tell you which of your religious and cultural forefathers spoke with me? Did I communicate with Abraham? Yes. Did I communicate with Noah? No. In fact," he chuckled, "there was no Noah. I created that unusual boating parable to illustrate humankind's capability to transform their experience. Most people who speak about that story totally miss the message—and you might want to remember this when your planet is collapsing, humans have the capability, if they are disciplined and work together, to save this planet. As an aside, you can probably think of circumstances within your own time, when a metaphorical ark was sorely needed."

Aaron paused, glanced at a line of people waiting for coffee service. As he looked, another employee entered the café, walked up to the barista machine and started making drinks.

Aaron looked back at me. "But returning to your question, for me to give you a list of names of those with whom I communicated—and another list of those with whom I didn't—well, those would be very long lists. And it would be a wasted effort because, in the final analysis, a useful message can be distorted into a message of ignorance and a wise person can produce a statement of truth without any assistance from me. You have to evaluate the message—what it means to you—rather than focusing upon who delivered it. No allegory is so magical, so truthful, that it cannot be twisted into a meaningless fairy tale."

I interrupted. "But how about prayer? Do you hear the prayers of each person who prays? Do you ever respond to those prayers?"

"Do I hear each prayer? The flow of prayer is part of the consciousness of the universe—as am I. So, in a sense, each prayer comes to me. But the value of a prayer begins and ends within the individual who prays. If a person prays to win a football game, it is an empty indulgent prayer. Nothing comes from it. When a person's prayer inspires them to stretch themselves, that prayer often is heard within the person's heart— and the person is able to answer their own prayer. If someone prays for something extraordinary that actually happens, either that person has answered their own prayer or the happening bore no relationship to the prayer. But prayer can and often does concentrate one's life force on an idea or on an outcome. It can help someone find understanding, compassion or the courage to act. Prayer for relief from misfortune or oppression gives hope. But prayer that asks for misery to occur to other people only diminishes the person who is praying."

Aaron offered a gentle smile and said, "I can anticipate your next couple of questions. First of all, no, I never initiate miracles that magically resolve the challenges a person faces. Each person is the only master of their fate. Humans must develop the skills to fully embrace and respond to life. What I give often are lessons in wisdom. Those who have wisdom know better how to respond to the challenges they face."

He paused, took a deep breath and exhaled. "But your second question needs a more expansive response. Life's challenges are not evenly distributed, Joseph, not at all. Some people face much more adversity than others. I know that doesn't seem fair. But fairness is a human concept—not without merit—but just not the way of the universe. However, even when a person's circumstances are overwhelming, there are more available paths forward than that person may recognize. Meanwhile, those who face fewer life challenges should never congratulate themselves on their skill, their efforts or their merit. Nor should they believe God favors them. Likewise, those who are forced to navigate difficult trials should not assume that God hates them—or believe they are being punished for any reason. Life is terribly uneven. Each person must cope with the opportunities as well as the challenges they are given." He paused before adding, "And continue to pursue as much harmony as possible."

Aaron looked at me intently. "The universe is complex, Joe. As we have discussed before, it works in ways you cannot comprehend—or imagine—and in ways I will not try to explain. Each life is, in itself, a complex puzzle. There is always an extraordinarily wide array of solutions to each set of challenges and opportunities. Every person must focus on putting their puzzle together from the pieces they are able to identify."

For a couple of minutes, Aaron looked down and was silent. Then, he looked up and said, "A moment ago, you asked about prayer. Prayer is different things to different people at different times. Prayer can be an excellent means of visualizing how the pieces of one's life might fit together. It can be a mechanism for dispelling stress when the elements in one's life don't appear to fit into a whole. Prayer can be a means of coming to understand one's circumstances—or a tool for evolving an individual's belief system to take on the challenges being faced. But once a path is discovered, once it is explored, calling a successful outcome a miracle is a mistake. God does not give solutions. While faith may be a basis for hope, it is never a substitute for a rigorous search for a solution—or the courage and discipline needed to implement it."

*****

Aaron looked out the window. I followed his example. It was still raining. Cars splashed through puddles as they raced toward their drivers' destinations. People of all descriptions moved past us, heads down, often carrying umbrellas. Some of them glanced into the coffee shop, sometimes even looking directly at us.

After about five minutes of silence, Aaron said, "This morning, you wanted me to share information about holy men and holy books. You wanted me to reveal my role in their works. You were curious whether I spoke to primitive men and women who dwelled in caves? Was I the basis for the Greek Gods? Did I inspire the Aztec ceremonies? Were Hinduism, Buddhism, Taoism, Islam, Christianity and Judaism results of my communications?"

He sighed, shook his head and chuckled. "Yes, Joseph. I was initially involved with each of those belief systems. I gave inspiration in different ways; to varying degrees. That being said, once I share a thought, it is owned—and then changed—by the men or women to whom I have communicated. The ideas are no longer mine. These individuals share those ideas with others. The concepts evolve and change over time as they are interpreted by teachers, priests, zealots and philosophers. In each of those belief systems, the ideas I shared evolved significantly after I let go of them. But it is up to you—to other human beings—to evaluate what parts of those religions, those philosophies, have value to you—and which ones don't. The parts you select are available to you to solve your puzzle of your life."

Aaron stopped speaking. I was behind in my notes and wrote madly for several minutes—trying to accurately document his words.

*****

When I looked up, Aaron said, "Today's conversation will be shorter than our others. Don't rush home. It would serve you well to take the rest of our time to contemplate what was said today as well as what we have spoken about in prior meetings. Go for a walk. Enjoy the beauty of the day. Think about the universe, the questions you've asked and the answers you have received. I will meet you here next week, same time."

He stood up, walked behind the counter and began taking orders for lattes, cappuccinos and americanos. For a few minutes, I watched him skillfully making coffee drinks. He knew what he was doing.

I left the coffee shop and was totally surprised to see the rain had stopped and the sky had cleared. I contemplated the morning's conversation while walking through the cool, fresh air that often follows a rain. As I returned to my car, I looked up at the sky. There was a full rainbow.

Even though it had been a short encounter, it had been satisfying. My confidence was growing that these meetings with an assorted cast of characters—whoever they were—were turning out to be worthwhile.

9: What is the Purpose of Art?

Spring had sprung and I had been spending quite a bit of time weeding, planting, pruning and enjoying the beginning of a new growing year. My unusual set of meetings with people claiming to be God was nearing closure. The meetings had been fascinating, the conversations interesting, but I was ready to return to my normal free time routines.

*****

I had been looking forward to that Sunday's meeting. Our subject was something I care a lot about—the arts. I parked my car a half-mile north of Paesano's and enjoyed a pleasant stroll through fresh morning air on my way to the coffee shop. As I walked, I studied the beautifully landscaped yards I passed along the way.

A middle-aged black man wearing a colorful dashiki was walking toward me. After giving me a warm smile, he said, "Good morning, Joseph."

I returned the smile saying, "Good morning."

He said, "Today, you can call me Veltry." He looked around and added, "It's such a fresh spring morning. Let's stretch our legs a little while we touch upon this area in which humans have been bold and visionary."

I smiled and said, "Sounds good."

"Let's head north." Veltry said. "And don't bother to pull out your pen and notebook. Just listen. You'll remember my words when you sit down to document them."

We headed back in the direction from which I had come. I was relieved to not have to take notes, to be able to focus on listening instead of recording every word.

Veltry jumped into the day's topic. "Humans spend a lot of time organizing, analyzing and categorizing all sorts of crap. They construct convoluted systems to organize their collective judgements—their so-called facts. Human beings are so damn confident that these facts are objective and accurate that they want to immortalize them in systems that they expect will be permanent. But wondrous as all those facts and systems are, they're pretty subjective."

Veltry chuckled. "Most humans believe their knowledge of the world around them is accurate, impartial and open-minded. What I find so amusing is that the same people who swear they are so damned objective describe everyone around them who has different facts and systems as ignorant or just plain wrong."

I realized Veltry was right.

After walking a block in silence, he moved back into his lecture. "The systems I referenced—scholars call them *the sciences*—are supposed to be fundamental truths of the universe. But scientists constantly update those truths. They replace old outdated facts with new improved facts. When this happens, the scientists explain that previous generations of facts were based on flawed assumptions and incorrect observations. But their new judgements about the universe, (you can trust them, of course) are all accurate. I don't mean to demean the role of scientists or of science. Science contributes a great deal to the quality of human life. But let's be frank. Even though their products are the most precise of all human perceptions, they are still imperfect. I spoke about the limitations of human perception tools in our first and second meetings. The inherent limitations of human perception and logic are sizeable. And as a result, objectivity, as demonstrated by science, is quite subjective."

Veltry grinned after he said that.

He went on, "This strong human desire to try to reach conclusions about the nature of the world extends to every aspect of human perceptions. It's true in economics, history, ethics, culture and political science. The way it works is that a human expert announces that he or she has reached the pinnacle of knowledge in an area. In the months that follow, some expert in the next continent, nation or university challenges those conclusions. I am not trying to say there is not great value in many of these studies. Some are extraordinary and offer real value to humans. I am just being up front in saying that knowing the true nature of things is not something that humans are gonna pull off—ever."

Veltry paused, then added. "But don't get me wrong, Joe. Given the limited tools available to those who have pursued understanding the mysteries of your world, many discoveries that have been made are noble and worthwhile. Developing the polio vaccine, discovering that the earth is not the center of the universe, coming to understand global economics—these and untold other discoveries uncovered by dedicated researchers represent extraordinary efforts and offer substantial value. But to say that scientific research has discovered useful tools is vastly different from saying that humanity has learned the fundamental nature of the universe."

Veltry's voice took on a surprising level of passion, "Only one component of human culture makes no pretense of objectivity. That area proudly doesn't deny its subjectivity—it embraces it. This area is the qualitative abstraction of human experience—the arts. The lack of pretense of objectivity in the fine arts gives a much-needed balance to civilization. Throughout history, humanity has stepped beyond its economic, scientific and other belief systems to express itself though the arts."

Veltry turned toward me and said, "You ask me about the significance of art? You wonder why I care about the arts? Art is how humans define themselves. Art, more than any other factor, separates humanity from other earthly animal species. If I care about humans at all, I care about the arts."

I was taken aback by Veltry's passion. I was accustomed to hearing constant criticism of mankind—some of it pretty nasty. But this was different. Veltry had just expressed profound respect for humanity.

I was surprised how good that felt!

*****

Veltry said nothing for two blocks. We continued on our promenade past an assortment of gorgeous gardens and classic homes.

When he did speak again, he continued where he had left off. "In creating art, humans have achieved—do achieve—their finest moments. Humans are unique on this planet in the diverse manners in which they communicate. But the arts are the avenues through which individuals speak from their hearts. Fine arts—song, story, clothing, painting, sculpture, performance, dance, food and architecture—are the ways in which cultures assert who they are."

Veltry's powerful speaking style was a refreshing change from the more conservative oratory of his fellow stand-ins for God. But while his positive statements about fine arts added to what the others had conveyed on previous Sundays, his perspectives about the inherent faults of human beings proved to be consistent with the others.

"There is a huge difference," he said, "between the arts and the sciences. Scientists create definitions that, while having immediate practical value, offer humanity a false sense of confidence and certainty. In the arts, no such pretense is made. Rather than denying the subjectivity of their experience; in the fine arts, humans celebrate and fully embrace the uncertainty, joy, anger, fear and every other human emotion that marks their lives. It is no surprise that art is always found in religious sanctuaries. Sculpture, stained-glass, painting, music, dance and other forms of artistic expression allow those who seek God to express and appreciate what is otherwise beyond their reach. In this way, the arts provide otherwise unavailable paths for individuals and communities to pursue harmony in a world which is beyond their ability to understand or control."

We walked past a classic white brick Cape Cod with green shutters. On both sides of the home were large red-flowered camelia shrubs. The flowerbeds on either side of its front porch seemed like explosions of snowdrops, crocuses, daffodils, tulips, and hyacinths. The front lawn had been recently mowed and, in a front corner of the yard, a flowering cherry was in full bloom.

"I appreciate that you enjoy gardening," Veltry said. "Growing plants is a wonderful avenue of artistic expression."

Veltry stopped, turned toward me and looked me squarely in the eye. His dark eyes twinkled as he said, "I realize that most of our conversations have focused upon your desire to *know* things. Many of my answers have emphasized that what you seek to know is beyond your reach. Human beings live in a world that is illusory. Art, however, is a means for humans to find peace and balance in spite of that uncertainty—to discover a road to harmony in the face of chaos. Art isn't just about joy. It doesn't only celebrate beauty. Art can express sorrow. It addresses helplessness. In so doing, art can alleviate the pain in a person's heart. When art expresses true emotion, it validates the innermost feelings of the artist—and of her or his audiences."

We began to walk again. A light breeze was blowing toward us. I took a deep breath and let it out slowly. This conversation was definitely validating.

*****

"In these sessions," Veltry went on, "I have tried to share insight into how the universe is bigger than you understand rather than to advise you on how to cope with life. But today, I will give you some advice. Every person, including you, can benefit from exploring some form of artistic expression. Too many people never attempt to create art because they believe they lack the ability."

Veltry looked down and shook his head slowly as he said, "That is such a tragedy. If the purpose of art is to express your heart, then refraining from expression—fearing that others will judge you as being without skill—that ends up being a denial of the message in your heart. It becomes a refusal to accept the fullness of your own unique life experience."

I thought about that. In college, I'd refused to take an art course. I explained to my friends that there was no point in taking the course because I had no talent. And now that my kids have left home, our piano sits unused because I am afraid that if I took piano lessons, others would laugh at my beginner's skill. Veltry was also right about gardening. Working in the yard was one of the most satisfying parts of my life. I looked over at Veltry. He was watching me as I pondered his comments.

Veltry continued. "Human beings also benefit from art created by others. Viewing, listening, partaking and reading the creations of others is enriching. In a world in which so many are isolated and alone, art is a wonderful means of bridging gaps between people. Enjoying other people's art is a way to understand how others have reconciled themselves to life's uncertainties."

*****

After strolling past picturesque neighborhoods, well-crafted early twentieth century homes and carefully landscaped yards, we arrived at a residential park where we sat down on a bench. We'd walked a lot. When I checked my watch, I saw it was noon. I wondered if the day's discussions were over.

However, Veltry had more to say. "Art is the expression of the heart, Joe. Artifice is a formulaic process that does not express real emotions. The difference between artifice and art is similar to the one between seduction and love. Only one of them speaks to or from the heart. Unfortunately, many in your civilization don't understand this dichotomy."

The tenor of Veltry's speech became more severe, more like some of the conversations I had had with his fellow-Gods on previous Sundays.

There was fire in his eyes as he said, "Your civilization produces an abundance of artifice. Most of your television, commercial music, popular literature and other formula driven cultural programming enriches no one. Media is not art unless its creator has spoken from the heart—responding to the uncertainty and emotion of their lives. One of the great tragedies of your modern times is that so much free time is wasted on addictive commercially driven artifice. Instead of creating harmony that enriches people, commercial media steals from the human experience."

*****

Veltry stood up. "Follow me," he said. "I want to show you a couple of things that have meaning—things that will help you understand harmony and give you insight into what I am saying. He led me across the park to a viewpoint overlooking Puget Sound. We looked out at the large expanse of water, at clouds moving across a blue sky and, in the distance, at the snowcapped Olympic Mountains.

Then he said, "C'mon," and led me to another side of the park where a white picket fence surrounded a stately brick home. He pointed at a large window on the home. Through it, I saw a woven Native American blanket hanging on an interior wall. The blanket's heavy tapestry was red, black, gray and white. Its design was simple, abstract and powerful.

"In the natural beauty of the sky, sea and mountains—and in that Navajo blanket—you see examples of harmony. Didn't viewing each put more peace into your heart than anything I said today? Didn't they offer more completeness than any idea I shared? You can't intellectually understand beauty. But you can know it."

I liked that thought.

Veltry reminded me that the following Sunday would be our final meeting. We would meet at the library.

He wished me a good day and walked off.

10: What is Humanity's Future?

In the days after each Sunday's meeting, I reviewed and completed my notes from the most recent conversation. While I had no recordings, I was surprised at the clarity with which I was able to recall the discussions. Even without notes from a couple of the meetings, I was able to accurately document our conversations. Several times, my wife asked me what I was doing. I told her I was putting together a short book that she would find interesting. I promised to share the manuscript with her as soon as it was completed. She was pleased with that and I felt good because I hadn't lied.

*****

It was Sunday again. I was sitting in the library conference room with Jeff Anderson. It had been almost ten weeks since I had met him. During that period, I had become comfortable with his (or her) changing physical characteristics and unusual messages. As I waited for Jeff to speak, I wondered if he would suggest we have a few additional meetings.

As I should have anticipated, Jeff began by addressing my unstated question. "Since this is our last meeting, Joe, I want to thank you. I've enjoyed getting together and appreciate how intently you've listened. You have worked diligently on your meeting notes. They are clear, concise and accurate."

I was flattered, but once again thrown off kilter because I hadn't shown him—or anyone—my draft manuscript that was located in my password protected home computer.

"Continue to work on the document. Your summaries will turn into a well written piece if you continue to stay true to what was said, allowing my words to retain their simplicity. Your memories of our conversations will remain fresh. Be patient. Take as much time as you need before you share it with others. I am trying to communicate something simple. Any attempt to make it complex will compromise the fabric of its truth. But I do have a suggestion. Go ahead and turn it into a novel. If you put our conversations into that format, it will reduce the temptation of others to accuse you of pretending to be speaking for God— which of course, everyone in these modern times knows is crazy."

After saying that, he launched into a lecture. "Today, you want me to tell you about the future of humanity. Your request is consistent with the questions and expectations you've had for all of our meetings. You get to the bottom line. You are so American, so modern—and often—so impatient."

He laughed softly. "My experience with humans has been like watching children who are more interested in a reward for completion of a task than in the thoroughness of the process or the quality of the product. Patience has rarely been the strong suit of human beings. It is a shame that meditation is not the favored approach of the time and civilization in which you live."

Jeff was silent for a while before continuing. "Antonio Stradivarius's violins would not make such sweet sounds today if he hadn't loved every moment of their fabrication three centuries ago. Stradivarius never worried whether he would be famous after he died. He just loved the art of making a violin. He always immersed himself in the creation of the one violin upon which he was working."

This was interesting. I was wondering how Anderson would connect a violin to mankind's future. However, I had learned to let the lectures proceed. Each Sunday, he or she ended up responding to my topic. I just had to be patient and listen.

"Antonio didn't just create violins. Antonio found God as he crafted musical instruments from pieces of wood. Humanity's challenge for the future is to behave more like Stradivarius. If humans can find anything approaching his level of patience and selflessness; if they can employ his sort of focus as communities work together to repair the earth; then humankind may achieve its greatest success. If human efforts are shortsighted, self-centered, or without love for the nature of this planet, the outcome will be dire. You want to know the future of humankind? What do you think it will be—and why?"

I was taken aback by his turning my question back to me. I had learned that oftentimes his or her questions were rhetorical. I waited. Jeff also waited. Finally, I realized he was not going to proceed until I had responded.

I took a deep breath and went for it. "I'll be honest, Jeff. It appears humans have not been able to find peace in this world—not peace between humans—not peace with nature. I am not confident that humanity will be around in two hundred years. In any case, we have a heavy price to pay for how we have corrupted the earth's bounty."

I paused, took a deep breath, exhaled and stopped speaking for a minute while I collected my thoughts. Then I said, "I'm afraid we will not be able to change our ways sufficiently to survive."

Anderson was silent. He looked out the conference room window. His look grew distant. His eyes seemed cold—his pupils becoming small dots.

He turned to me and said, "Your analysis is interesting. Your conclusions may turn out to be accurate. The question I have for you is this: Why even try? If all is for naught, why try? What is your reason for getting up in the morning? What are you hoping to achieve?"

I said nothing. Minutes passed. A deafening silence filled the room. Again, I realized Jeff was going to wait until I responded.

I spoke from the heart. I didn't know what I was going to say until the words were out of my mouth. "Why do I get up in the morning? What am I trying to achieve? I am not certain—no—I just don't know. I was really looking forward to this—to our final conversation. I hoped you would give me an answer to this question. I was anticipating your insight. I hoped you would say something that was encouraging—that would be inspiring for all humans."

Anderson closed his eyes, took a long breath in and slowly exhaled. When he opened his eyes, he looked kindly at me and said, "I would think that when you get up in the morning and see the sun rise; that in itself, would be encouraging. When you see a flower bloom in the spring or a child learn to walk, you would realize that incredible things are constantly happening around you. I don't see you thinking these thoughts. You take those wonderful little things for granted. But you shouldn't, Joseph."

He was quiet again for a couple of minutes. I sat and watched him. He shook his head—almost sadly—this time when he looked at me, I saw a lot of kindness.

"Many small things," Jeff said, "done in concert with one another can accomplish extraordinary results. Human beings may not be able to understand the breadth of life or the complexity of the universe, but each human being has the capacity to affect his or her own destiny. If humans cooperate with one another, they have the capacity to amaze themselves as to what they can accomplish—how they can affect the destiny of their planet—and their species."

Jeff paused, giving me a chance to write down his statement.

When I finished writing and looked up, Jeff said. "Humanity has faced horror in the past. You haven't. Your life, Joseph, has been relatively without tumult. You did not experience the black plague in the fourteenth century. Half of humanity died in a period of a few decades!"

Jeff took another deep breath, letting it out before saying, "Your tribe—the United States—has not been subject to rape and murder—at least not since the attempted genocide of your indigenous populations and the slavery of African people of color. And you personally, Joseph, have not been the victim of those horrible exercises in violence. You haven't been hungry. You've never been homeless. Your life has been relatively safe and secure."

I waited. He looked at me for several minutes before continuing. "However," he said, "all of humanity is now faced with a number of significant challenges—challenges of its own making. Resolution will not come from knowing what the future will bring. Passive fatalism would result in a disastrous future—as would the behavior which typifies modern governmental and political institutions—egotistical grandstanding by leaders, blame games and competing efforts by tribes will only accelerate disaster. Humanity's future has not been decided. Thoughtful and cohesive behavior can change the tide. But the challenges humans face must be addressed quickly. Let me be more explicit. There are things that humanity can do today that will affect tomorrow. It is within human beings' power to affect their destiny, to make peace with nature, to gain wisdom and patience—to find harmony."

Nothing was said in that library conference room for at least ten minutes. I watched Jeff. He did not return my gaze. He just looked out the window.

Finally, he turned back to me and said, "Antonio Stradivarius loved the sound of the violin so much that he learned to love making a violin even more than listening to its sound. But his efforts were never about Antonio Stradivarius. His passion began with an appreciation of the music that a well-crafted violin could produce. Over the years, his love grew for the pieces of spruce, maple and willow from which he crafted his art. His affection for his tools—for his lacquer—never stopped growing. But most of all, what happened inside of him was a love of careful and patient process. Antonio Stradivarius learned to love making a violin more than listening to the sweet sound it emoted once it was complete. But one thing is for certain, Joseph—it was never, ever, about Antonio."

In a soft voice Jeff said, "For thousands of years, across your planet, holy people have practiced chanting as a method of finding inner peace. Chanting has the pleasant resonant effect of creating harmonics— multiple frequencies or vibrations which rise beyond the foundational sound emitted by the person who chants. Those who chant achieve an inner peace when these harmonics occur. However, those who chant really don't understand how that inner peace occurs. They just chant."

*****

It seemed like we were done with our conversations. Nothing was said for about five minutes. The quiet felt good—peaceful. For an instant, I fell back into wondering if this was all real. Might it be a dream—or a flight of insanity? Had I been conned. Was I acting like a fool?

Then it hit me. It didn't make a bit of difference. I was gaining an insight into life that was worthwhile. What I had learned had meaning to me as a person—someone wanting to better understand who I am and what humans are in the context of a larger universe.

*****

But Anderson had more to say. "You did not ask the one question I had anticipated. You have faithfully stayed with your original list of themes for our interviews. But I know there were times when you wanted to ask that question—and you didn't."

Anderson was quiet for a moment before saying, "I will ask that question for you, Joseph. How could God have allowed the Holocaust?"

I said nothing. A question can be so fundamental to who you are that it becomes a shadow over your life. Over the past few weeks, I would sometimes wake up in the middle of the night and lay in bed wondering if I should ask that question. I had thought about bringing up the Holocaust several times during our meetings. I just hadn't had the courage. I had even considered asking God that question during that final meeting. But I wasn't able to. I was too uncomfortable with the pain attached to it.

My father was raised a German Jew. In 1939, in order to get out of Nazi Germany, he asked acquaintances in England to invite him for a visit. Months later, when he left for England, his goodbye to his mother was a final farewell. She remained in Frankfurt. In 1942, the Gestapo deported her to the Majdanek death camp near Lublin, Poland. She was murdered there. My father also lost uncles, aunts, cousins and many friends to the Nazi death camps. He never got over it.

I was born after World War II ended. But my childhood was dominated by my father's extraordinary grief. He refused to believe in a God that could allow the Holocaust to have happened.

I sat there, in front of Jeff or God or whomever. I waited and listened. This was personal.

Jeff took a deep breath, emphatically exhaled, then spoke. "There are no chosen people, Joseph. Throughout human history, certain tribes have shown leadership—or borne the brunt of hate and violence. The Jewish people have experienced both. Were they chosen for their role? No. Is their history special because they have provided and endured so much? Absolutely! But there are many other peoples who have suffered, who have shown fortitude and leadership, who were special—and who suffered. The story of the European Holocaust is not unique in history—or even in modern times. The hate that some humans have nurtured—the violence that that hate produced—it's just plain tragic."

Jeff stopped for a moment and sighed. "The belief that if a person is pure of heart, she or he will not suffer—well, that is just not the way the world is. Explaining away the suffering of those who died in gas chambers by saying that God punished them is also wrong."

Jeff leaned forward and looked directly into my eyes. I returned his gaze.

"As I have referenced before, many religions teach that God punishes. That is just not correct. Humanity is more in control of its destiny than humans have ever been willing to accept or admit. Individuals suffer because other humans persecute them. Civilizations could create a better world. The fact that they haven't—well, this is not a world without pain. Not for any living creature. This is a universe that includes both harmony and disharmony; a world in which humanity's destiny is created by humans—not by God."

He put his hands over mine as he said, "In answer to your father's question, in answer to yours, God did not create the Holocaust. Humans created it. There is nothing I can say that will undo the pain of the Holocaust—not for you, not for your father, and not for the millions of others whose hearts are full of sadness and anger because of pain they experienced—from the Holocaust or from any of the other cruel, inhumane actions that have been committed throughout time—by humans."

I absorbed what he had said. I knew it was true. I understood that while there were many things which I liked about civilization; violence, greed and inhumanity were also fundamental to our species and our histories.

*****

Jeff had one more statement to make. "You came to these interviews distrusting me totally. But you also hoped I would give you a key to life. I have gained some of your trust. But I have definitely not given you a key to life. Such a simplistic solution to the human dilemma does not exist. Life is a riddle with no simple answer. It is a unique puzzle for each person. If there is a goal to pursue, it is to increase harmony in the universe while putting your puzzle together."

God stood up and said in a soft voice, "Thank you for listening to me, for documenting my thoughts and for trying to understand. I wish you nothing but the best."

And with that said, he walked out of the room.